COMPLETE HEALTHY VEGETARIAN COOKBOOK

Innovative vegetarian recipes for the adventurous cook

Edited by
Janet Swarbrick
& Jenny Stacey

Quantum
Books

AN OCEANA BOOK

Published by
Quantum Publishing Ltd.
6 Blundell Street
London N7 9BH

ISBN 1-86160-487-4

QUMCVC

Printed in Singapore by
Star Standard Industries (Pte) Ltd.

The material in the book previously appeared in:
Mediterranean Vegetarian Cooking
Healthy Vegetarian Cooking
Low-Fat Vegetarian Cooking

CONTENTS

MAIN DISHES

SIDE DISHES

INTRODUCTION

There is now such a selection of fruits, vegetables and pulses in almost every supermarket, greengrocers or farm shop, be it in the centre of the city or way out in the country! Given this astonishing variety it is quite easy to see that, for anyone wishing to follow a vegetarian diet, there is a wealth of ingredients readily available to provide colourful dishes of varied tastes and textures. In short, the modern vegetarian diet is fresh and exciting – no wonder more and more people are enjoying healthy, high fibre vegetarian eating.

Yet vegetarianism is not a new culinary trend – it was a way of life for many of the great thinkers and philosophers of the Ancient World, and has been advocated for thousands of years by sects of both the Hindu and Buddhist faiths, for whom all animal life is considered sacred.

A diet for a healthy world

Religion had great influence on all areas of people's lives for many centuries and, while it still does for some, it is now as likely to be emotional or environmental issues that make people stop and think about their diet as much as matters of spirituality.

Many teenagers turn to vegetarianism, largely due to peer pressure but also because the realisation that the lambs and piglets seen enjoying the sunshine are destined for the table. The lack of detailed answers to questions arising from intensive farming methods, notably the BSE crisis, has also persuaded many to embrace vegetarianism.

Vegetarian or Vegan?

Many people refer to themselves as vegetarians if they do not eat red meat, but this is inaccurate. No vegetarians eat any animal flesh, which includes poultry and fish as well as red and white meats. Vegans, those who follow the strictest vegetarian diet, will not eat anything at all that is derived from animals – no cheese, butter or any milk-based foods; indeed some also refuse honey, which they do not believe should be taken from the bees. A creative vegan diet is one of the great culinary challenges.

Lacto-vegetarians do not eat any foods that involve the slaughter of animals, so they will not eat eggs although they do include dairy products such as cheese and milk, whereas octo-lacto vegetarians will eat eggs.

There are growing numbers of would-be vegetarians who eat fish. This is especially true of those who lead a very active life, or who are just converting to vegetarianism. Colloquially referred to as "demi-veg", this is a compromise in terms of true vegetarianism but one which many parents are happy to accept for their young people.

LEFT A diet rich in fresh vegetables is highly recommended.

A healthy vegetarian diet

Many so called "modern" or Western diseases are inevitably linked to our over-processed, fatty convenience diet. Lifestyle also plays a large part in such illnesses. Fatty foods and lack of exercise undoubtedly contribute to heart disease, whereas a shortage of dietary fibre leads to many digestive disorders and diseases.

Animals are not the only source of dietary protein – cereals, nuts and beans all contain secondary, or vegetable, proteins. Very few, however, contain all the essential amino acids necessary to recreate the protein that we eat as body protein. It is therefore of paramount importance that a vegetarian diet should be varied, incorporating all types of cereals and beans. The classic example of this is that bread made from wheat flour is incomplete in terms of essential amino acids – toast it and put a helping of baked beans on top and you have a protein-rich snack!

Fibre – the key to healthy eating

Fibre is the most important part of the vegetarian diet, the most effective weapon against the malaise brought on by the mediocrity of processed foods. Dietary fibre forms the cell walls of plants – the super-structure or skeleton. It is unique to plants and it is therefore easy to see that a diet rich in animal proteins and fat, but lacking in cereals and vegetables can be almost totally lacking in fibre – but why should this matter.

Fibre is essential for the efficient working of the digestive system and therefore the processing of our food.

A pappy diet is easy to eat and presents little intestinal challenge. Indeed, much of the progress in the early days of the "food industry" was aimed at making eating "easier" by refining foods. However, intestinal inactivity causes disorders and disease. In the less developed countries of the world where the staple diet is rice, lentils and vegetables there is disease, but much of it is associated with vitamin deficiencies rather than with a lack of dietary fibre.

To keep healthy it is important to cook with, and eat, as many unprocessed foods as possible, which leads inevitably to a high fibre diet. What is amazing is that, even among meat-eaters, the foods that we think of as starches or carbohydrates (fibre foods) often contribute a significant amount of protein to the diet – between 20 and 30 per cent of the protein in an average diet comes from potatoes. Cut out the animal proteins, which automatically leads to a reduction in fat, increase fibre-rich foods and a healthy diet is easily achieved.

Extra proteins for vegetarians

Vegetable protein foods are becoming more and more common, and there is quite a movement in agriculture towards soya, a high protein crop which can be used as solids or liquid and which produces a much better protein yield per hectare than livestock. This is regarded as one of the most plausible ways of increasing the quality of the international diet.

Tofu, a recent introduction to many Westerners but a staple protein food of the Chinese for many thousands of years, also has a valuable place in the vegetarian diet. It is bean curd and is also known as soyabean curd. It is best fresh when the texture is firm. Natural or smoked tofu may be sliced and quickly fried, then added to salads and other vegetable dishes, or beaten into fillings for pies and flans.

Other vegetable protein foods are being developed as "chunks", sausages or mince. They often have little, if any, flavour of their own, but readily absorb flavorsome marinades and sauces. Combining these with foil-baked squashes and corns makes a vegetarian barbecue so much more interesting than the average meat-eaters feast of burnt sausages and chicken pieces.

Robust flavours for robust foods

Many beans and legumes respond deliciously to clever and inventive use of herbs and spices. Roasting your own whole spices, such as cumin and coriander seeds, in a dry pan and grinding them just before use achieves the best possible flavour. Alternatively, buy small quantities of ground spices and replace them regularly. Dried seasonings are only at their best for a few months and certainly cease to pack a punch after a year.

Fresh herbs have the best flavour, but they can be very expensive, especially if you have to buy them from a supermarket. Keep freeze-dried herbs for emergencies but, if you are lucky enough to have a herb garden, do try to use fresh leaves whenever possible. Herbs for garnish should be chopped and added at the last moment, to retain colour and immediacy of flavour. Even if you do not have a garden it is a good idea to grow some herbs in pots on your windowsill – some varieties, such as basil, are indeed better this way than outside in an unreliable climate.

One of the most exciting trends in popular cooking in the last few years has been the use of salsas as salad garnishes, and these work especially well with bean-based dishes. A mixture as simple as an orange, tomatoes, spring onions and roasted mustard seeds with fresh coriander and a chopped chilli can add the most exciting explosion of colour, texture, and flavour to a casserole or bake.

Cutting down on fat

You should never aim to eradicate fat from your diet completely as it is essential for a healthy skin, for energy and to keep the organs of the body "well-oiled" by providing a protective coating. Too much fat, however, causes problems – it is one of the food groups that can, unfortunately, be stored if we eat too much!

The benefits of fruit as a substitute for refined fatty desserts are numerous. Not only do they have no fat, but they supply essential vitamins, minerals and fibre.

There is a certain amount of fat present in most foods, but especially in animal proteins. Cheese is a very concentrated fatty food and it is better to use less of a mature cheese than a larger amount of a mild one. It is essential not to be tempted to eat cheese two or three times a day – there are plenty of other ways of adding flavour to dishes, and many other foods that can be used for sandwich fillings and snacks.

Vegetarians often use nuts, but these contain large amounts of oil and therefore fat. Recipes that call for browned or fried nuts should be adapted to dry-frying nuts in a non-stick pan, or grilling them, so that extra oil is not required during cooking.

The use of plenty of fresh herbs can adequately compensate for any loss of dairy flavour on a low-fat diet.

Fats for flavour

Fats, which include soft and solid spreads and oils, can be divided into three categories: *saturated fats* which are normally hard at room temperature and are mainly derived from meat or meat products, although coconut oil and palm oil also fall into this category. These fats tend to raise the blood cholesterol level above that which is required for healthy tissues and hormones, leading to atherosclerosis and possible heart attack.

Polyunsaturated fats are usually vegetable products, liquid at room temperature and which have a neutral effect on cholesterol. They include the most common vegetable oils, and the soft margarines which are clearly labelled as polyunsaturated, e.g. sunflower.

Monounsaturated fats are the group that has received most publicity in recent years as olive oil is a key member of the group. Avocados and peanut oil also fall into this group, which has been found to have a neutralising, beneficial effect on cholesterol in the blood.

It is therefore reasonable to suggest that olive oil is good for you and should be included in a healthy diet. It is not, however, an invitation to drown all foods in this delicious nectar which is still a fat and contains plenty of calories.

Stir-frying for health

Gone are the days of kids being packed off to college with a microwave cooker – now they want a wok! Stir-fries are cheap and filling, incorporating a good variety of colourful, crisp vegetables and spicy sauces, all cooked in just a spoonful or two or oil. The secret of a good stir-fry is to have all the ingredients ready, cut into similar-sized pieces, before you begin cooking. Heat the wok until hot, add a little oil and then the vegetables. Stir for two to three minutes, then serve with rice or noodles.

Treats and variety

Just because a pudding or cake is made with fibre-rich ingredients, doesn't make it healthy. Many such foods have a high proportion of fats and sugars and are absolutely loaded with calories. We all want treats occasionally, but where an active teenager will be able to devour these foods without adding an inch to the waistline, for most of us even high-fibre treats will have an unfortunate effect on the figure, and should be kept for special occasions only.

A healthy vegetarian diet is colourful, creative, and fun. Dare to try your own exotic combinations of foods and push the boundaries of conventionality by combining salads, salsas and flavourings with robust and satisfying casseroles and bakes. And remember, a healthy diet is a varied diet, so enjoy experimenting with the enormous variety of fresh and dried foods that are now available.

FAT AND CHOLESTEROL CONTENT OF FOODS		
	fat g PER 100g	cholesterol mg PER 100g
Milk and Milk Products		
Milk, cows'		
fresh, whole	3.8	14
long-life, whole	3.8	14
fresh, skimmed	0.1	2
Milk, goats'	4.5	–
Cream		
light	21.2	66
heavy	35.0	100
Cheese		
Camembert-type	23.2	72
Cheddar-type	33.5	70
Cheddar-type, low-fat, average	16.0	varies
Cheddar-type, with sunflower oil	33.0	more than 5
cottage cheese, low-fat	4.0	13
cream cheese, full fat	47.4	94
Yogurt, low fat		
plain	1.0	7
fruit	1.0	6
Fats and Oils		
Butter, salted	82.0	70
Lard	99.0	70
Low-fat spread	40.7	trace
Margarine, hard	81.0	varies
Margarine, sunflower oil	80.0	less than 5
Vegetable oils	99.9	trace
Eggs		
Whole , raw	10.9	450
White, raw	trace	0
Yolk, raw	30.5	1260
Dried	43.3	1780

BRIGHT BREAKFASTS

APRICOT YOGURT CRUNCH

SERVES 4

A variation on a Scottish dish, the crunchy porridge oats, spicy yogurt, and lightly poached fruit make an attractive morning dish.

275 g (10 oz) apricots, pitted

45 ml (3 tbsp) honey

50 g (2 oz) porridge oats, toasted

2.5–5 g (½–1 tsp) ground ginger

275 g (10 oz) low-fat natural yogurt

≈ Place the apricots in a pan with 150 ml (¼ pint) water and 15 ml (1 tablespoon) of the honey. Cook for 5 minutes until softened and drain.

≈ Mix the oats and remaining honey in a bowl. Stir the ginger into the yogurt.

≈ Alternately layer the fruit, yogurt and oat mixtures into serving glasses. Chill and serve.

NUTRITION FACTS	
Serving Size 1 (162g)	
Calories 140	Calories from Fat 18
	% Daily Value
Total Fat 2g	2%
Saturated Fat 1g	4%
Monounsaturated Fat 0.5g	0%
Polyunsaturated Fat 0.2g	0%
Cholesterol 4mg	1%
Sodium 78mg	3%
Total Carbohydrate 28g	9%
Dietary Fibre 2g	7%
Sugars 23g	0%
Protein 5g	0%

Per cent daily values are based on a 2000 calorie diet

BANANA ENERGY

SERVES 4

If you can't face a full breakfast in the morning, take your energy in a glass with this nutritious drink.

4 large bananas, peeled and cut into chunks

15 ml (1 tbsp) lemon juice

300 ml (½ pint) low-fat natural yogurt

300 ml (½ pint) skimmed milk

30 ml (2 tbsp) honey

lemon slices and mint sprigs, for garnish

≈ Place all the ingredients in a food processor or blender. Liquidize for 1 minute until smooth. Pour into tall serving glasses, garnish, and serve immediately.

NUTRITION FACTS	
Serving Size 1 (276g)	
Calories 210	Calories from Fat 18
	% Daily Value
Total Fat 2g	3%
Saturated Fat 1g	5%
Monounsaturated Fat 0.3g	0%
Polyunsaturated Fat 0.1g	0%
Cholesterol 6mg	2%
Sodium 91mg	4%
Total Carbohydrate 44g	15%
Dietary Fibre 3g	11%
Sugars 34g	0%
Protein 8g	0%

Per cent daily values are based on a 2000 calorie diet

Apricot Yogurt Crunch ▶

CRUNCHY MORNING SCONES

MAKES 14

*These lightly spiced scones are delicious served piping hot with cinnamon yogurt,
thus eliminating the necessity for butter.*

115 g (4 oz) self-raising flour

115 g (4 oz) wholemeal self-raising
flour

pinch of ground cinnamon

pinch of ground nutmeg

25 g (1 oz) polyunsaturated
margarine

50 g (2 oz) all-bran cereal

15 g (1 tbsp) chopped, skinned
hazelnuts

45 g (3 tbsp) sultanas

1 egg

90 ml (6 tbsp) skimmed milk

For the cinnamon yogurt

150 ml (¼ pint) low-fat natural
yogurt

1.5 g (¼ tsp) ground cinnamon

2.5 ml (½ tsp) honey

NUTRITION FACTS	
Serving Size 1 (48g)	
Calories 113	Calories from Fat 27
	% Daily Value
Total Fat 3g	5%
Saturated Fat 1g	3%
Monounsaturated Fat 1.3g	0%
Polyunsaturated Fat 0.7g	0%
Cholesterol 16mg	5%
Sodium 191mg	8%
Total Carbohydrate 19g	6%
Dietary Fibre 3g	12%
Sugars 4g	0%
Protein 4g	0%

Per cent daily values are based on a 2000 calorie diet

≈ Preheat the oven to 200°C (400°F, Gas 6). Place the flours and spices in a bowl and rub in the margarine to resemble fine breadcrumbs. Stir in the all-bran, nuts and sultanas. Stir in the egg and milk and bring together to form a soft dough.

≈ Knead the dough on a lightly floured surface and cut into eight 7.5 cm (3 in) rounds with a cutter. Brush the tops with a little extra milk and place on a floured baking sheet. Bake for 20 minutes until risen and golden. Mix together the yogurt ingredients and serve with the warm scones. Sprinkle with extra cinnamon to garnish, if desired.

GRILLED PINK GRAPEFRUIT

SERVES 4

A quick, simple breakfast; it may be speedy but its flavour is sensational.

2 Florida pink grapefruit
30 ml (2 tbsp) honey
pinch of ground allspice
mint sprigs to garnish (optional)

≈ Cut the skin away from the grapefruit, remove any remaining pith and cut each grapefruit into quarters. Place the quarters in a heatproof shallow dish.

≈ Mix together the honey and allspice and spoon over the grapefruit pieces. Cook under the grill for 5 minutes. Serve garnished with mint if desired.

NUTRITION FACTS	
Serving Size 1 (134g)	
Calories 69	Calories from Fat 0
	% Daily Value
Total Fat 0g	0%
Saturated Fat 0g	0%
Monounsaturated Fat 0.0g	0%
Polyunsaturated Fat 0.0g	0%
Cholesterol 0mg	0%
Sodium 1mg	0%
Total Carbohydrate 18g	6%
Dietary Fibre 1g	6%
Sugars 16g	0%
Protein 1g	0%

Per cent daily values are based on a 2000 calorie diet

PORRIDGE WITH POACHED FRUIT

SERVES 4

A quick porridge which can be made in advance or the night before. Hearty and filling, the poached fruit sets it off perfectly.

175 g (6 oz) porridge oats

1.05 litres (1¾ pints) skimmed milk

175 g (6 oz) plums, halved, pitted
    and sliced

120 ml (8 tbsp) honey

≈ Place the porridge oats in a pan with the milk. Bring to the boil, reduce the heat and simmer for 5 minutes, stirring until thickened.

≈ Meanwhile, place the plums in a saucepan with 30 ml (2 tablespoons) of honey and 150 ml (¼ pint) water. Bring to the boil, reduce heat and simmer for 5 minutes until softened. Drain well.

≈ Spoon the porridge into individual bowls and top with the poached plums. Serve hot with the remaining 90 ml (6 tablespoons) of honey.

NUTRITION FACTS	
Serving Size 1 (359g)	
Calories 310	Calories from Fat 18
	% Daily Value
Total Fat 2g	2%
Saturated Fat 1g	7%
Monounsaturated Fat 0.3g	0%
Polyunsaturated Fat 0.3g	0%
Cholesterol 5mg	2%
Sodium 183mg	8%
Total Carbohydrate 66g	22%
Dietary Fibre 2g	7%
Sugars 46g	0%
Protein 11g	0%

Per cent daily values are based on a 2000 calorie diet

BREAKFAST HASH

MAKES 4

For a speedier breakfast, cook the potatoes for this tasty dish the evening before and store in a sealed bag in the refrigerator until required.

675 g (1½ lbs) peeled, cubed
    potatoes

15 ml (1 tbsp) sunflower oil

1 red pepper, seeded and halved

1 green pepper, seeded and halved

2 tomatoes, diced

115 g (4 oz) open cap mushrooms,
    peeled, quartered

30 g (2 tbsp) fresh chopped parsley

ground black pepper

≈ Cook the potatoes in boiling water for 7 minutes, drain well. Heat the sunflower oil in a large frying pan, add the potatoes and cook for 10 minutes, stirring.

≈ Chop the red and green peppers and add to the pan with the tomatoes and mushrooms. Cook for 5 minutes, stirring constantly, add the chopped parsley, season to taste and serve.

NUTRITION FACTS	
Serving Size 1 (277g)	
Calories 179	Calories from Fat 36
	% Daily Value
Total Fat 4g	6%
Saturated Fat 0g	2%
Monounsaturated Fat 1.6g	0%
Polyunsaturated Fat 1.6g	0%
Cholesterol 0mg	0%
Sodium 88mg	4%
Total Carbohydrate 34g	11%
Dietary Fibre 4g	15%
Sugars 6g	0%
Protein 4g	0%

Per cent daily values are based on a 2000 calorie diet

Breakfast Hash ▶

FRUIT KEBABS

SERVES 4

The perfect way to present fresh fruit, these lightly grilled kebabs with a hint of mint make a refreshing start to the day.

30 g (2 tbsp) caster sugar

2 mint sprigs, plus extra for garnish

1 papaya, halved, seeded and chopped into 5 cm (2 in) squares

1 mango, stoned and chopped into 5 cm (2 in) squares

1 star fruit, sliced

2 kiwi fruit, thickly sliced

≈ Soak four wooden skewers in water for 30 minutes. Remove when ready to use. Place the sugar, mint and 150 ml (¼ pint) water in a pan. Heat gently to dissolve the sugar and then bring to the boil until reduced by half. Discard the mint.

≈ Thread the fruit onto the skewers, alternating the varieties. Brush with the syrup and grill for 10 minutes, turning and brushing until heated through. Serve hot, garnished with mint.

HASH BROWN POTATOES WITH BAKED BEANS

SERVES 6

These golden potato cakes are served with a spicy bean dish, and are perfect for mopping up the delicious juices. Make the bean dish in advance and keep in the refrigerator until morning. Simply heat the beans in a pan over a gentle heat.

≈ Drain the soaked beans and rinse well under cold water. Drain and put in a large saucepan with 475 ml (16 fl oz) of water. Bring the beans to the boil and boil rapidly for 10 minutes. Reduce the heat to a simmer, cover and cook for 1 hour or until the beans are cooked, topping up the water if necessary. Drain the beans and return them to the pan. Stir in the vegetable stock, dried mustard, onion, molasses, tomatoes, tomato purée and basil. Season well and cook for 15 minutes or until the vegetables have cooked.

≈ Meanwhile, make the potato cakes while the beans are cooking. Cook the potatoes in boiling water for 20 minutes or until soft. Drain well and mash with the milk.

≈ Add the onion and garlic, mixing well and form into twelve equal-sized cakes. Brush a non-stick frying pan with the oil and warm over a medium heat. Cook the potato cakes for 15–20 minutes, turning once until golden brown. Serve hot with the baked beans.

NUTRITION FACTS	
Serving Size 1 (260g)	
Calories 154	Calories from Fat 9
	% Daily Value
Total Fat 1g	1%
Saturated Fat 0g	0%
Monounsaturated Fat 0.0g	0%
Polyunsaturated Fat 0.2g	0%
Cholesterol 0mg	0%
Sodium 12mg	0%
Total Carbohydrate 37g	12%
Dietary Fibre 6g	23%
Sugars 25g	0%
Protein 1g	0%

Per cent daily values are based on a 2000 calorie diet

For the baked beans

225 g (8 oz) dried navy beans,
    soaked overnight

150 ml (¼ pint) vegetable stock

2.5 g (½ tsp) dried mustard

1 onion, chopped

30 ml (2 tbsp) dark molasses

225 g (8 oz) tomatoes, peeled,
    chopped

15 ml (1 tbsp) tomato purée

15 g (1 tbsp) fresh chopped basil

ground black pepper

For the potato cakes

675 g (1½ lbs) peeled, cubed
    potatoes

30 ml (2 tbsp) skimmed milk

1 onion, chopped

1 garlic clove, crushed

10 ml (2 tsp) sunflower oil

Hash Brown Potatoes with Baked Beans

NUTRITION FACTS	
Serving Size 1 (194g)	
Calories 241	Calories from Fat 18
	% Daily Value
Total Fat 2g	4%
Saturated Fat 0g	2%
Monounsaturated Fat 0.7g	0%
Polyunsaturated Fat 0.9g	0%
Cholesterol 0mg	0%
Sodium 125mg	5%
Total Carbohydrate 46g	15%
Dietary Fibre 8g	30%
Sugars 3g	0%
Protein 11g	0%

Per cent daily values are based on a 2000 calorie diet

6 slices wholemeal bread, with crusts removed

15 g (1 tbsp) polyunsaturated margarine

1 red pepper, halved and seeded

1 green pepper, halved and seeded

2 tomatoes, chopped

50 g (2 oz) low-fat Cheddar cheese, grated

2 egg whites, beaten

475 ml (16 fl oz) skimmed milk

ground black pepper

NUTRITION FACTS	
Serving Size 1 (165g)	
Calories 112	Calories from Fat 18
	% Daily Value
Total Fat 2g	4%
Saturated Fat 1g	3%
Monounsaturated Fat 1.0g	0%
Polyunsaturated Fat 0.7g	0%
Cholesterol 1mg	0%
Sodium 214mg	9%
Total Carbohydrate 16g	5%
Dietary Fibre 2g	9%
Sugars 5g	0%
Protein 8g	0%

Per cent daily values are based on a 2000 calorie diet

75 g (3 oz) wholemeal flour

115 g (4 oz) plain flour

15 g (1 tbsp) baking powder

65 g (2½ oz) muesli

30 ml (2 tbsp) chopped dates

10 g (2 tsp) soft brown sugar

1 egg white, whisked

150 ml (¼ pint) skimmed milk

30 g (2 tbsp) polyunsaturated margarine, melted

NUTRITION FACTS	
Serving Size 1 (46g)	
Calories 119	Calories from Fat 27
	% Daily Value
Total Fat 3g	4%
Saturated Fat 1g	3%
Monounsaturated Fat 0.9g	0%
Polyunsaturated Fat 0.7g	0%
Cholesterol 0mg	0%
Sodium 170mg	7%
Total Carbohydrate 21g	7%
Dietary Fibre 1g	5%
Sugars 5g	0%
Protein 3g	0%

Per cent daily values are based on a 2000 calorie diet

BREAD PUDDING

SERVES 8

Renowned as a delicious, but fattening dish, this savoury bread pudding is the perfect example of adapting a recipe to low-fat without compromising on taste.

≈ Spread the bread with the margarine and cut each slice into four triangles by cutting on the diagonal.

≈ Place the peppers skin side uppermost on a rack and grill for 10 minutes until blackened. Place in a plastic bag with tongs, seal and let cool. Peel off the the skins and discard. Slice the peppers into thin strips.

≈ Layer the bread, peppers, tomatoes and half of the cheese in a large shallow ovenproof dish. Mix the egg white and milk together and pour over the bread. Allow to stand for 30 minutes.

≈ Sprinkle the remaining cheese over the dish and season. Cook in the oven at 170°C (325°F, Gas 3) for 45 minutes until set and risen. Serve hot.

BREAKFAST MUFFINS

MAKES 12

Breakfast wouldn't be breakfast without muffins. This healthy version gives you all the goodness you'd want from an old favourite.

≈ Place the flours, baking powder, muesli, dates and brown sugar in a bowl. In a separate bowl, mix together the egg white, milk, and margarine. Add to the dry ingredients all at once. Stir gently.

≈ Spoon the mixture into eight muffin cases to two-thirds full. Bake in the oven at 220°C (425°F, Gas 7) for 20–25 minutes until risen and golden. Serve warm.

Bread Pudding ▶

225 g (8 oz) strawberries, hulled and
   chopped
150 ml (¼ pint) cranberry juice
30 ml (2 tbsp) honey
2.5 g (½ tsp) ground ginger
475 ml (16 fl oz) sparkling mineral
   water
ice and mint sprigs to serve
4 whole strawberries, for garnish

NUTRITION FACTS

Serving Size 1 (265g)

Calories 85	Calories from Fat 0
	% Daily Value
Total Fat 0g	0%
Saturated Fat 0g	0%
Monounsaturated Fat 0.0g	0%
Polyunsaturated Fat 0.2g	0%
Cholesterol 0mg	0%
Sodium 3mg	0%
Total Carbohydrate 21g	7%
Dietary Fibre 2g	9%
Sugars 20g	0%
Protein 1g	0%

Per cent daily values are based on a 2000 calorie diet

For the scones

50 g (2 oz) wholemeal flour
5 g (1 tsp) baking powder
5 g (1 tsp) caster sugar
1 medium egg, beaten
85 ml (2½ fl oz) skimmed milk
1 green dessert apple, cored and
   chopped
15 g (1 tbsp) raisins

For the yogurt sauce

150 ml (1¼ pints) low-fat natural
   yogurt
2.5 g (½ tsp) ground cinnamon
5 ml (1 tsp) honey

NUTRITION FACTS

Serving Size 1 (122g)

Calories 131	Calories from Fat 18
	% Daily Value
Total Fat 2g	3%
Saturated Fat 1g	4%
Monounsaturated Fat 0.7g	0%
Polyunsaturated Fat 0.3g	0%
Cholesterol 55mg	18%
Sodium 368mg	15%
Total Carbohydrate 23g	8%
Dietary Fibre 3g	10%
Sugars 11g	0%
Protein 6g	0%

Per cent daily values are based on a 2000 calorie diet

STRAWBERRY COCKTAIL

SERVES 4

*A refreshing breakfast cocktail with a sparkle. It is as quick and easy to make
as it is to drink.*

≈ Place the strawberries, cranberry juice, honey and ginger in a food processor and blend for 30 seconds until smooth.

≈ Add the sparkling mineral water, ice and mint. Pour into glasses, garnish, and serve immediately.

APPLE DROP SCONES

SERVES 4

*This healthy version of a breakfast favourite is filled with chunks of crisp apple
which are complemented by the cinnamon spiced yogurt sauce.*

≈ Sift the flour and baking powder for the scones into a mixing bowl and stir in the sugar. Make a well in the centre and beat in the egg and milk to make a smooth batter. Stir in the apple and raisins, mixing well.

≈ Brush a heavy based non-stick frying pan with a little oil and warm over medium heat. Divide the batter into eight equal portions and drop four portions into the pan, spacing them well apart. Cook for 2–3 minutes until the top of each drop scone begins to bubble. Turn the scones over and cook for 1 minute. Transfer to a warmed plate and keep hot while cooking the remaining four scones.

≈ Mix the yogurt sauce ingredients together in a bowl and serve with the hot drop scones.

Apple Drop Scones ▶

SPICED PEARS

SERVES 4

The aroma from this dish is almost as good as the taste, and all part of the enjoyment. If liked, serve with a spoonful of natural yogurt or cottage cheese.

4 large ripe pears, peeled, halved and cored

300 ml (½ pint) mango juice

1 cinnamon stick, crushed

2.5 g (½ tsp) grated nutmeg

45 g (3 tbsp) raisins

30 g (2 tbsp) soft brown sugar

≈ Place the pear halves in a pan with the fruit juice, spices, raisins and sugar. Heat gently to dissolve the sugar and then bring to the boil.

≈ Reduce the heat to a simmer and cook for a further 10 minutes until the pears are softened. Serve hot with the syrup.

NUTRITION FACTS	
Serving Size 1 (259g)	
Calories 204	Calories from Fat 18
	% Daily Value
Total Fat 2g	3%
Saturated Fat 0g	0%
Monounsaturated Fat 0.1g	0%
Polyunsaturated Fat 0.2g	0%
Cholesterol 0mg	0%
Sodium 21mg	1%
Total Carbohydrate 50g	17%
Dietary Fibre 7g	27%
Sugars 37g	0%
Protein 1g	0%

Per cent daily values are based on a 2000 calorie diet

SPICY FRUIT SALAD

SERVES 4

Dried fruits are filled with goodness and have a delicious, concentrated flavour of their own. With many varieties now available it is easy to mix delicious combinations to create your personal favourite fruit salad.

115 g (4 oz) dried apricots

50 g (2 oz) dried peaches

50 g (2 oz) dried mango

50 g (2 oz) dried pears

115 g (4 oz) dried stoned prunes

5 g (1 tsp) ground cinnamon

900 ml (1½ pints) orange juice

3 mint sprigs

150 ml (¼ pint) low-fat natural yogurt

grated zest of 1 orange

≈ Place the fruits in a bowl and add the cinnamon and orange juice. Cover and leave to soak overnight.

≈ Place the contents of the bowl in a saucepan with the mint and bring to the boil, reduce the heat to a simmer and cook for 20 minutes until the fruits have softened. Cool and transfer to the refrigerator. Cover until required.

≈ Remove the mint from the salad. Mix together the yogurt and orange zest. Serve with the fruit salad.

NUTRITION FACTS	
Serving Size 1 (370g)	
Calories 368	Calories from Fat 18
	% Daily Value
Total Fat 2g	3%
Saturated Fat 0g	2%
Monounsaturated Fat 0.5g	0%
Polyunsaturated Fat 0.3g	0%
Cholesterol 2mg	1%
Sodium 36mg	2%
Total Carbohydrate 89g	30%
Dietary Fibre 8g	31%
Sugars 70g	0%
Protein 6g	0%

Per cent daily values are based on a 2000 calorie diet

Spiced Pears ▶

APPETIZERS, SOUPS AND SALADS

2 flour tortillas

For the filling

115 g (4 oz) spinach, stems removed

4 spring onions, sliced

25 g (1 oz) low-fat vegetarian
    Cheddar cheese, grated

a pinch of ground coriander

1 small celery stick, trimmed and
    sliced

50 g (2 oz) drained, canned corn

1 carrot, peeled and grated

For the sauce

150 ml (¼ pint) skimmed milk

10 g (2 tbsp) cornflour

150 ml (¼ pint) vegetable stock

4 pickled jalapeño chillies, sliced

50 g (2 oz) low-fat vegetarian
    cheese, grated

15 ml (1 tbsp) tomato purée

15 g (1 tbsp) fresh chopped basil

basil or coriander sprigs to garnish

Vegetable Enchiladas

NUTRITION FACTS	
Serving Size 1 (221g)	
Calories 183	Calories from Fat 36
	% Daily Value
Total Fat 4g	6%
Saturated Fat 1g	6%
Monounsaturated Fat 1.0g	0%
Polyunsaturated Fat 0.7g	0%
Cholesterol 8mg	3%
Sodium 652mg	27%
Total Carbohydrate 25g	8%
Dietary Fibre 3g	12%
Sugars 5g	0%
Protein 13g	0%

Per cent daily values are based on a 2000 calorie diet

VEGETABLE KEBABS

SERVES 6

Perfect for vegetable lovers. This colorful combination of vegetables, marinated in vermouth, is served on a bed of bulghar wheat lightly flavored with cilantro.

≈ Prepare all the vegetables and place in a shallow dish. Mix together the vermouth, oil, 2 tablespoons of the lemon juice, garlic, half of the cilantro and half of the lemon rind. Pour over the vegetables, cover and marinate for 2 hours.

≈ Meanwhile, place the bulghar wheat in a bowl, pour over 1¼ cups boiling water. Let sit for 30 minutes or until the water is absorbed. Drain if necessary and stir in the remaining lemon juice and cilantro. Season.

≈ Remove the vegetables from the marinade and thread onto four skewers. Broil for 10 minutes, turning until cooked through. Serve the bulghar wheat with the kabobs.

1 zucchini, sliced
1 yellow bell pepper, seeded and cubed
4 baby corn, halved
4 button mushrooms
1 small red bell pepper, seeded and cubed
½ cup vermouth
1 tbsp olive oil
4 tbsp lemon juice
1 garlic clove, minced
2 tbsp fresh chopped cilantro
grated rind of 1 lemon
⅔ cup bulghar wheat
ground black pepper.

VEGETABLE ENCHILADAS

SERVES 4

This is a vegetarian version of the Mexican dish. Here, flour tortillas are filled with a mixture of crunchy vegetables, rolled and baked with a spicy tomato sauce. Pickled jalapeño chiles have been used as they are milder in flavor than fresh chiles.

≈ Blanch the spinach for the filling in boiling water for 2–3 minutes. Drain well and put in a mixing bowl with the scallions, cheese, coriander, celery, corn, and carrot.

≈ Spoon half of the filling along one edge of each of the tortillas. Roll up the tortillas and cut in half. Put in a shallow ovenproof baking dish, seam side down.

≈ For the sauce, blend 4 tablespoons of the skim milk to a paste with the cornstarch. Heat the remaining milk and vegetable broth in a saucepan and stir in the cornstarch paste, jalapeño chiles, half of the cheese, and the tomato paste.

≈ Bring the sauce to a boil, stirring until thickened. Cook for 1 minute and pour over the tortillas in the dish. Sprinkle the remaining cheese on top and cook in the oven at 350°F for 30 minutes or until the sauce is bubbling and the cheese has melted. Garnish with cilantro or basil and serve with a small salad.

NUTRITION FACTS	
Serving Size 1 (209g)	
Calories 209	Calories from Fat 27
	% Daily Value
Total Fat 3g	5%
Saturated Fat 0g	2%
Monounsaturated Fat 1.7g	0%
Polyunsaturated Fat 0.3g	0%
Cholesterol 0mg	0%
Sodium 50mg	2%
Total Carbohydrate 35g	12%
Dietary Fiber 5g	19%
Sugars 2g	0%
Protein 4g	0%

Percent daily values are based on a 2000 calorie diet

40 g (1½ oz) bulgur wheat

675 g (1½ lb) spinach, stems
    removed

45 ml (3 tbsp) vegetable stock

1 onion, chopped

2 garlic cloves, crushed

15 g (1 tbsp) fresh chopped oregano

15 g (1 tbsp) fresh chopped thyme

10 ml (2 tsp) cider vinegar

1 egg, beaten

30 g (2 tbsp) fresh chopped
    coriander

50 g (2 oz) low-fat cheese, grated

6–8 large lettuce leaves

NUTRITION FACTS

Serving Size 1 (138g)

Calories 66	Calories from Fat 18
	% Daily Value
Total Fat 2g	2%
Saturated Fat 0g	2%
Monounsaturated Fat 0.4g	0%
Polyunsaturated Fat 0.2g	0%
Cholesterol 29mg	10%
Sodium 120mg	5%
Total Carbohydrate 8g	3%
Dietary Fibre 3g	13%
Sugars 1g	0%
Protein 6g	0%

Per cent daily values are based on a 2000 calorie diet

SPINACH PÂTÉ

SERVES 8

This is a baked pâté which needs to be made well in advance of serving as it requires chilling after cooking. Be sure when draining the spinach to press out as much water as possible otherwise the mixture will be too wet. This recipe would be suitable for a lunch for four if sliced and served with salad or a tomato sauce.

≈ Cook the bulgur wheat in boiling water for 15 minutes or until swollen and cooked. Drain well. Wash the spinach and cook in a saucepan until it begins to wilt. Drain very well and chop finely.

≈ Heat the stock in a saucepan and cook the onion and garlic for 2–3 minutes until beginning to soften. Add the bulgur wheat, oregano, thyme and vinegar and cook for 5 minutes. Remove the saucepan from the heat and stir in the egg, chopped coriander, cheese and spinach.

≈ Line a 900 g (2 lb) loaf tin with the lettuce leaves, allowing them to overhang the edge. Spoon the spinach mixture into the pan and fold the lettuce leaves over the top to cover the mixture completely.

≈ Cover the tin and cook the pâté in the oven at 180°C (350°F, Gas 4) for 45–60 minutes or until firm. Allow to cool before transferring to the refrigerator to chill for 2 hours. Unmould the pâté, slice and serve with hot toast and a small salad.

4 large, thick slices of crusty bread

2 garlic cloves, crushed

15 ml (1 tbsp) low-fat
    polyunsaturated spread, melted

4 ripe tomatoes, peeled and chopped

15 ml (1 tbsp) tomato purée

4 stoned black olives, chopped

ground black pepper

basil sprigs to garnish

NUTRITION FACTS

Serving Size 1 (162g)

Calories 123	Calories from Fat 27
	% Daily Value
Total Fat 3g	5%
Saturated Fat 0g	2%
Monounsaturated Fat 0.0g	0%
Polyunsaturated Fat 0.0g	0%
Cholesterol 0mg	0%
Sodium 265mg	11%
Total Carbohydrate 20g	7%
Dietary Fibre 2g	9%
Sugars 4g	0%
Protein 4g	0%

Per cent daily values are based on a 2000 calorie diet

MEDITERRANEAN TOASTS

SERVES 4

These bite-sized hot open sandwiches are delicious as a snack or appetizer. Use a small crusty bread such as Italian ciabatta or a French stick if preferred, using eight slices in place of four. Be sure to cook these just before serving for full flavour.

≈ Toast the slices of bread under the grill for 2 minutes each side. Mix the garlic and low-fat spread together and drizzle on to one side of the toasted bread.

≈ Mix the tomatoes, tomato purée and olives together, season, and spoon on to the toast. Cook under the grill for 2–3 minutes or until hot. Remove the toasts from under the grill and cut in half. Garnish with basil and serve.

Mediterranean Toasts ▶

CRUDITÉES WITH CHILLI TOMATO DIP

SERVES 4

O ne of the simplest yet most popular appetizers, an array of colourful, crisp vegetables served with a delicious dip is hard to resist.

2 celery sticks, trimmed and cut into
  eight pieces
1 green pepper, halved, seeded and
  cut into strips
1 carrot, cut into julienne sticks
3 cherry tomatoes
40 g (1½ oz) mangetout

For the dip

300 ml (½ pint) low-fat natural
  yogurt
15 ml (1 tbsp) tomato purée
60 ml (4 tbsp) low-fat mayonnaise
1 green chilli, chopped
15 g (1 tbsp) fresh chopped parsley

≈ Prepare all the vegetables. Mix together the dip ingredients and place in a serving bowl.

≈ Place the bowl on a serving platter and arrange the vegetables around the dip. Serve immediately.

BAKED POTATO SKINS

SERVES 4

A lways a firm favourite, remember to prepare the skins a day in advance for ease and speed. Pop them into the oven to warm them through before serving.

≈ Scrub the potatoes and place on a baking sheet. Cook in the oven at 200°C (400°F, Gas 6) for 1 hour or until soft. Remove and cool. Cut the potatoes in half lengthways and scoop out the centres with a teaspoon, leaving a 1 cm (½ in) thickness shell. Sprinkle the skins with salt and place the potatoes in the oven for 10 minutes or until crisp.

≈ Mix the yogurt dip ingredients together. Mix together the mustard sauce ingredients. Finally mix the tomato salsa ingredients together. Place each dip in a separate bowl and cover until required. Serve with hot potato wedges.

NUTRITION FACTS	
Serving Size 1 (205g)	
Calories 105	Calories from Fat 18
	% Daily Value
Total Fat 2g	4%
Saturated Fat 1g	4%
Monounsaturated Fat 0.3g	0%
Polyunsaturated Fat 0.6g	0%
Cholesterol 4mg	1%
Sodium 330mg	14%
Total Carbohydrate 17g	6%
Dietary Fibre 3g	10%
Sugars 10g	0%
Protein 5g	0%

Per cent daily values are based on a 2000 calorie diet

4 medium baking potatoes

For the yogurt dip

150 ml (¼ pint) low-fat natural
    yogurt
2 garlic cloves, crushed
15 g (1 tbsp) spring onions, sliced

For the mustard sauce

150 ml (¼ pint) low-fat natural
    yogurt
10 ml (2 tsp) wholegrain mustard
1 jalapeño chilli, chopped

For the tomato salsa

2 medium tomatoes, chopped
45 g (3 tbsp) red onion, finely
    chopped
15 g (1 tbsp) fresh chopped parsley
1 green pepper, seeded and chopped
dash of sugar

Baked Potato Skins

NUTRITION FACTS	
Serving Size 1 (414g)	
Calories 325	Calories from Fat 18
	% Daily Value
Total Fat 2g	3%
Saturated Fat 1g	4%
Monounsaturated Fat 0.5g	0%
Polyunsaturated Fat 0.3g	0%
Cholesterol 4mg	1%
Sodium 107mg	4%
Total Carbohydrate 70g	23%
Dietary Fibre 7g	28%
Sugars 16g	0%
Protein 10g	0%

Per cent daily values are based on a 2000 calorie diet

VEGETABLE AND BEAN SOUP

SERVES 8

This is a really hearty soup, filled with goodness. It may be made with any selection of vegetables you have to hand and is perfect for making ahead and freezing.

1.75 litres (3 pints) vegetable stock

1 onion, sliced

225 g (8 oz) potato, cubed

2 carrots, peeled and sliced

1 parsnip, peeled, cored, and chopped

1 leek, sliced

140 g (4½ oz) baby corn, sliced

2 garlic cloves, crushed

5 g (1 tsp) curry powder

5 g (1 tsp) chilli powder

450 g (16 oz) can red kidney beans, drained

450 g (16 oz) can borlotti or pinto beans, drained

ground black pepper

30 g (2 tbsp) fresh chopped parsley

≈ Heat 150 ml (¼ pint) of the stock in a large saucepan and cook the onion, potato, carrots, parsnip, leek, corn and garlic for 5 minutes.

≈ Add the curry and chilli powders with the remaining stock and bring the soup to the boil. Reduce the heat and simmer for 20 minutes or until the vegetables are tender. Add the drained beans and cook for a further 10 minutes. Season to taste and garnish with parsley before serving with crusty bread.

VEGETABLE JAMBALAYA

SERVES 4

This is a classic Caribbean dish, usually made with spicy sausage, but this vegetarian version packs just as much of a punch and tastes wonderful.

≈ Cook the rices in boiling water for 20 minutes or until cooked. Drain well.

≈ Meanwhile, place the aubergine pieces in a colander, sprinkle with the salt and leave to stand for 20 minutes. Wash and pat dry with absorbent kitchen paper.

≈ Put the aubergine, onion, celery and stock in a non-stick pan and cook for 5 minutes, stirring. Add the garlic, corn, beans, carrots, tomatoes, tomato purée, creole seasoning and chilli sauce. Bring the mixture to the boil, reduce the heat and cook for a further 20 minutes until the vegetables are just cooked. Stir in the drained rice and cook for a further 5 minutes. Garnish with parsley and serve.

NUTRITION FACTS	
Serving Size 1 (348g)	
Calories 275	Calories from Fat 18
	% Daily Value
Total Fat 2g	3%
Saturated Fat 0g	1%
Monounsaturated Fat 0.0g	0%
Polyunsaturated Fat 0.4g	0%
Cholesterol 0mg	0%
Sodium 980mg	41%
Total Carbohydrate 51g	17%
Dietary Fibre 11g	43%
Sugars 4g	0%
Protein 17g	0%

Per cent daily values are based on a 2000 calorie diet

45 g (1¾ oz) long grain white rice

40 g (1½ oz) wild rice

1 aubergine, sliced and quartered

5 g (1 tsp) salt

1 onion, chopped

1 celery stick, trimmed and sliced

175 ml (6 fl oz) vegetable stock

2 garlic cloves, crushed

40 g (1½ oz) baby corn

90 g (3½ oz) green beans, trimmed

175 g (6 oz) baby carrots

250 ml (8 fl oz) canned chopped
   tomatoes

20 ml (4 tsp) tomato purée

5 g (1 tsp) creole seasoning

5 g (1 tsp) chilli sauce

fresh chopped parsley to garnish

Vegetable Jambalaya

NUTRITION FACTS	
Serving Size 1 (228g)	
Calories 141	Calories from Fat 9
	% Daily Value
Total Fat 1g	2%
Saturated Fat 0g	1%
Monounsaturated Fat 0.1g	0%
Polyunsaturated Fat 0.5g	0%
Cholesterol 0mg	0%
Sodium 904mg	38%
Total Carbohydrate 29g	10%
Dietary Fibre 3g	11%
Sugars 3g	0%
Protein 6g	0%

Per cent daily values are based on a 2000 calorie diet

PUMPKIN SOUP WITH COURGETTES

SERVES 4

Replacing animal fats with sunflower oil significantly reduces cholesterol content of any dish. When only half of the vegetables are puréed, as in this recipe, the soup has a more interesting texture and a more appetizing appearance.

1 tbsp sunflower oil

1 medium onion, chopped

350 g/12 oz pumpkin or squash, peeled, seeded, and diced

225 g/8 oz carrots, diced

2 potatoes, peeled or scrubbed and diced

700 ml vegetable stock

2 courgettes, thinly sliced

freshly ground black pepper

Garnish

2 tbsp chopped parsley

≈ Place the oil and onion in a saucepan, and cook over medium heat for 2–3 minutes to soften the onion. Add the pumpkin or squash, carrots, potatoes, and stock. Bring to the boil, cover, and simmer for 15 minutes, or until the vegetables are nearly tender. Add the courgettes and cook for another 5 minutes.

≈ Purée half of the soup in a blender or food processor, stir the purée into the remaining soup, and season with salt and pepper to taste. Reheat the soup if necessary, and serve in individual bowls. Make sure that some of the courgette slices float on top to decorate the soup. Sprinkle with parsley and serve piping hot.

NUTRITION FACTS	
Amount per Serving	
Calories 135	Calories from Fat 27
	% Daily Value
Total Fat 3g	5%
Saturated Fat 0.5g	2.5%
Polyunsaturated Fat 2g	0%
Monounsaturated Fat 0.5g	0%
Cholesterol 0mg	0%
Sodium 22mg	1%
Total Carbohydrate 23g	8%
Dietary Fibre 5g	20%
Sugars 7g	0%
Protein 3g	0%

Percent daily values are based on a 2000 calorie diet

GAZPACHO

SERVES 4

A favourite soup of Southern Europe, gazpacho can have more bread added to make it more substantial.

450 g/1 lb large ripe tomatoes

1 large onion

2 cloves garlic

1 green pepper

1 red pepper

½ cucumber

2 slices wholewheat bread,
   crusts removed

3 tbsp olive oil

3 tbsp wine vinegar

285 ml/½ pt tomato juice

285 ml/½ pt water

salt and freshly ground black pepper

≈ Skin tomatoes, discard seeds and juice and chop the flesh. Peel and finely chop the onion and garlic. Remove pith and seeds from peppers; dice. Peel and dice the cucumber. Dice the bread.

≈ Put vegetables and bread in a large bowl, pour over the remaining ingredients, stir and season. Chill well – overnight is best for a good tasty soup.

≈ You can partly blend the soup if you wish, or blend all of it, in which case offer small bowls of chopped onions, tomatoes, peppers, cucumber and croutons as a garnish.

NUTRITION FACTS	
Amount per Serving	
Calories 188	Calories from Fat 80
	% Daily Value
Total Fat 9g	14%
Saturated Fat 1g	5%
Polyunsaturated Fat 1g	0%
Monounsaturated Fat 6g	0%
Cholesterol 0mg	0%
Sodium 290mg	12%
Total Carbohydrate 21g	7%
Dietary Fibre 7g	28%
Sugars 13g	0%
Protein 5g	0%

Percent daily values are based on a 2000 calorie diet

CREAMY CHESTNUT SOUP

SERVES 4

Chestnuts often replace beans in Mediterranean cooking and they are used in the same way as potatoes are elsewhere in Europe. Here they make a delicious, creamy winter soup, delicately flavoured with a little cinnamon.

450 mg/1 lb chestnuts unshelled or
350 mg/12 oz shelled

salt and freshly ground black pepper

1 thick slice of bread

4 tbsp olive oil

2 tbsp red-wine vinegar

625 ml/1¼ pt light stock

⅛ tsp cinnamon

NUTRITION FACTS	
Amount per Serving	
Calories 275	Calories from Fat 117
	% Daily Value
Total Fat 13g	20%
Saturated Fat 2g	10%
Polyunsaturated Fat 2g	0%
Monounsaturated Fat 9g	0%
Cholesterol 0mg	0%
Sodium 67mg	2.8%
Total Carbohydrate 37g	12%
Dietary Fibre 4g	16%
Sugars 6g	0%
Protein 3g	0%

Percent daily values are based on a 2000 calorie diet

≈ If unshelled, slash the chestnut shells in an x-shape across the fat part of the nut, drop into a pan and cover with cold water with a little salt. Bring to the boil and cook for 20 minutes. Let them cool (but leave under water).

≈ Peel the chestnuts, removing brown skin too.

≈ Fry the bread in the oil then put it in a blender or food processor and purée with the vinegar. Reserve a handful of coarse nuts (chopped) to add texture to the soup and add the rest to the blender, a little at a time, with some of the stock. Purée to a cream. Return the creamed soup to the pan, taste and season with salt and pepper. Flavour discreetly with the cinnamon. Add the chopped nuts, heat through and serve.

PASTA AND PEA SOUP

SERVES 4

A simplified version of Italian minestrone, *this recipe uses wholewheat pasta spirals which have a higher fibre content than regular pasta. You could substitute any other pasta shapes you have.*

1 medium onion, chopped

1 clove garlic, crushed

2 celery sticks, finely chopped

2 medium carrots, thinly sliced

1 bouquet garni

2 bay leaves

170 ml/6 fl oz tomato juice

600 ml/1 pt water

140 g/5 oz wholewheat pasta spirals

175 g/6 oz frozen peas

⅓ tsp mixed herbs

1 tsp paprika

salt

Garnish

few sprigs coriander or parsley
   (optional)

≈ Place the onion, garlic, celery, carrots, bouquet garni, bay leaves, tomato juice and half the water in a large saucepan. Bring to the boil, lower the heat, cover, and simmer for 5–6 minutes.

≈ Add the remaining water, pasta, peas, herbs and paprika. Bring to the boil and simmer for 8–10 minutes until the pasta is tender. Season to taste.

≈ Serve piping hot in individual bowls, garnished with fresh herbs if you wish.

NUTRITION FACTS	
Amount per Serving	
Calories 158	Calories from Fat 18
	% Daily Value
Total Fat 2g	3%
Saturated Fat 0.3g	1.5%
Polyunsaturated Fat 1g	0%
Monounsaturated Fat 0.2g	0%
Cholesterol 0mg	0%
Sodium 47mg	2%
Total Carbohydrate 28g	9%
Dietary Fibre 13g	52%
Sugars 8g	0%
Protein 10g	0%

Percent daily values are based on a 2000 calorie diet

CLEAR MUSHROOM SOUP

SERVES 4

This is a formal soup for special occasions. It has a strong mushroom flavour with the delicate addition of vegetables and pasta to create the contrasting textures.

25 g/1 oz dried mushrooms

600 ml/1 pt warm water

1 leek

1 carrot

80 g/3 oz conchigliette piccole (tiny pasta shells), cooked

salt and freshly ground black pepper

flat parsley leaves to garnish

≈ Place the mushrooms in the warm water, and leave to soak for about 30 minutes. Drain the mushrooms, reserving the liquid in a saucepan.

≈ Slice the mushrooms, and shred the leek and carrot. Add the vegetables to the mushroom stock and cook over a medium heat for about 10 minutes, until the vegetables are tender.

≈ Add the cooked pasta shells, and season with salt and freshly ground black pepper. Cook for a further minute. Serve garnished with parsley leaves.

NUTRITION FACTS	
Amount per Serving	
Calories 37	Calories from Fat 6
	% Daily Value
Total Fat 0.7g	3%
Saturated Fat 0.1g	0.5%
Polyunsaturated Fat 0.4g	0%
Monounsaturated Fat 0g	0%
Cholesterol 0mg	0%
Sodium 10mg	0.4%
Total Carbohydrate 5g	1.6%
Dietary Fibre 3g	12%
Sugars 3g	0%
Protein 3g	0%

Percent daily values are based on a 2000 calorie diet

PASTA BEAN SOUP

SERVES 4

A nutritious meal in itself – low-fat and full of protein. Serve with warm, crusty garlic bread.

2 tbsp olive oil

3 cloves garlic, crushed

4 tbsp chopped fresh parsley

175 g/6 oz dried wholewheat gnocchi piccoli (shells) pasta

3 1/6 pt vegetable stock

3 tbsp tomato paste

350 g/14 oz can mixed beans, such as borlotti, cannellini, etc

salt and freshly ground black pepper

freshly grated Parmesan cheese

≈ Heat the olive oil in a large saucepan, and sauté the garlic with the chopped parsley for about 2 minutes. Add the pasta and cook for 1–2 minutes, stirring constantly.

≈ Pour in the vegetable stock, and add the tomato paste. Bring to a boil, reduce the heat, then simmer for about 10 minutes, stirring occasionally, until the pasta is tender.

≈ Add the beans, and season with salt and freshly ground black pepper. Continue to cook for a further 5 minutes, then serve with a little freshly grated Parmesan cheese.

NUTRITION FACTS	
Amount per Serving	
Calories 338	Calories from Fat 90
	% Daily Value
Total Fat 10g	15%
Saturated Fat 1g	5%
Polyunsaturated Fat 1g	0%
Monounsaturated Fat 4g	0%
Cholesterol 3mg	1%
Sodium 432mg	18%
Total Carbohydrate 52g	17%
Dietary Fibre 11g	44%
Sugars 6g	0%
Protein 14g	0%

Percent daily values are based on a 2000 calorie diet

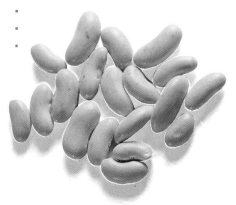

BROAD BEAN AND MUSHROOM SOUP

SERVES 4

A traditional farmhouse dish, this soup is high in both fibre and nutrients; the broad beans are a very good source of zinc and potassium.

4 oz (115 g) broad beans, soaked
    overnight in cold water

1 tsp sunflower oil

2 medium onions, chopped

2 celery stalks, sliced

½ lb (225 g) potatoes, peeled or
    scrubbed and diced

¼ lb (115 g) button mushrooms,
    trimmed and sliced

4 tbsp tinned corn drained

10 fl oz (300 ml) skimmed milk

salt and freshly ground black pepper

Garnish

2 tbsp chopped parsley

NUTRITION FACTS	
Amount per Serving	
Calories 195	Calories from Fat 27
	% Daily Value
Total Fat 3g	5%
Saturated Fat 0.5g	2.5%
Polyunsaturated Fat 2g	0%
Monounsaturated Fat 0.5g	0%
Cholesterol 2mg	0.6%
Sodium 110mg	4.5%
Total Carbohydrate 34g	11%
Dietary Fibre 8g	32%
Sugars 9g	0%
Protein 10g	0%

Percent daily values are based on a 2000 calorie diet

≈ Drain the beans and place them in a large saucepan covered with fresh water. Boil them rapidly for 10 minutes, then simmer them for 35–40 minutes until they are soft. Drain the beans and reserve 1 pint of the stock.

≈ Heat the oil in a large saucepan, and fry the onion over medium heat until it softens. Add the celery and potato, and cook for 2–3 minutes, stirring.

≈ Add the reserved stock and mushrooms, bring to a boil, then cover and simmer for 10 minutes. Add the beans, corn and milk, bring just to simmering point, and simmer for 2–3 minutes. Season to taste.

≈ Serve the soup in individual bowls, sprinkled with parsley.

ONION, LENTIL AND LEMON SOUP

SERVES 6

Barley and lentils are two Armenian favourites paired in this earthy soup. Served with warm cornbread, it would make a filling supper or lunch.

8 fl oz (250 ml) water

3 oz (75 g) pearl barley

1 tbsp tomato purée

3 pts (1½ l) vegetable stock

12 oz (340 g) lentils, rinsed and
 picked over

5 onions, sliced very thinly

1 tsp dried anise seeds

juice of 1 large lemon

large pinch of sweet paprika

pinch of cayenne pepper

salt and freshly ground black pepper

Garnish

12 paper-thin lemon slices

≈ Bring the water to a boil in a large enamelled or stainless steel saucepan. Stir in the barley, cover, and simmer over low heat for about 20–25 minutes, until the barley is just tender and the water has been absorbed. Stir in the tomato purée, vegetable stock, lentils, onions and anise. Bring to a boil, cover, and simmer over low heat for 1 hour, or until the lentils are soft.

≈ Stir in the lemon juice, paprika, cayenne pepper, and salt and pepper to taste, and simmer uncovered for a further 20 minutes. Pour the soup into heated bowls, and garnish each with two very thin slices of lemon.

NUTRITION FACTS	
Amount per Serving	
Calories 137	Calories from Fat 9
	% Daily Value
Total Fat 1g	1.5%
Saturated Fat 0.1g	0.5%
Polyunsaturated Fat 0.4g	0%
Monounsaturated Fat 0.1g	0%
Cholesterol 0mg	0%
Sodium 15mg	0.6%
Total Carbohydrate 27g	9%
Dietary Fibre 3g	12%
Sugars 3.5g	0%
Protein 7g	0%

Percent daily values are based on a 2000 calorie diet

GREEK POTATO SALAD

SERVES 4

Make this salad up to two days before eating it, keep it covered in the refrigerator, and forget about it until required. The flavours will be much stronger when it comes to serving.

900 g/2 lb small new potatoes, scrubbed

1 medium red onion, finely sliced into rings

50 g/2 oz kalamata olives

4 tbsp olive oil

2 tbsp red-wine vinegar

salt and freshly ground black pepper, to taste

1 tsp dried thyme

NUTRITION FACTS	
Amount per Serving	
Calories 278	Calories from Fat 117
	% Daily Value
Total Fat 13g	20%
Saturated Fat 2g	10%
Polyunsaturated Fat 1g	0%
Monounsaturated Fat 9g	0%
Cholesterol 0mg	0%
Sodium 307mg	13%
Total Carbohydrate 38g	13%
Dietary Fibre 4g	16%
Sugars 4g	0%
Protein 4g	0%

Percent daily values are based on a 2000 calorie diet

≈ Place the potatoes in a large saucepan and cover with boiling water. Bring back to the boil and cook for 20–25 minutes, or until the potatoes are tender. Drain and allow to cool slightly.

≈ Cut the potatoes into ½ cm/¼ in slices and arrange in a circular pattern on a serving plate, alternating the potato slices with the onion rings. Scatter the olives over the mixture.

≈ Combine the oil, vinegar, seasoning and thyme in a screw-top jar and shake well to mix. Pour the dressing over the salad. Cover and chill before serving.

CLASSIC GREEK SALAD

SERVES 4

The secret of this internationally famous salad is not in its method, but in its ingredients. You need the freshest of everything to create the feeling of lazy days in the Mediterranean sunshine.

2 large ripe tomatoes

½ cucumber, diced

1 green pepper, seeded and sliced into rings

50 g/2 oz kalamata olives

1 large red onion, finely sliced

175 g/6 oz feta cheese, cut into small cubes

finely grated zest and juice of ½ lemon

4 tbsp olive oil

1 tsp dried oregano

coarsely ground salt, to taste

≈ Cut the tomatoes into thin wedges and place in a medium-sized bowl. Add the cucumber, pepper and olives.

≈ Toss the salad together with half of the red onion slices and half of the cubed feta. Scatter the remaining onions and feta over the top of the salad.

≈ Sprinkle the lemon zest and juice over the mixture, drench with the olive oil, and season with the oregano and salt. Gently toss the salad once just before serving.

NUTRITION FACTS	
Amount per Serving	
Calories 258	Calories from Fat 200
	% Daily Value
Total Fat 22g	34%
Saturated Fat 8g	40%
Polyunsaturated Fat 2g	0%
Monounsaturated Fat 11g	0%
Cholesterol 31mg	10%
Sodium 920mg	38%
Total Carbohydrate 7g	2%
Dietary Fibre 3g	12%
Sugars 6g	0%
Protein 9g	0%

Percent daily values are based on a 2000 calorie diet

VEGETABLE SALAD

SERVES 6

In Scandinavia this salad, known as rosolli, *is very often eaten as a savoury pick-me-up on Christmas Eve morning.*

7 fresh beetroot

5 potatoes

7 carrots

2 apples

2 medium onions

3 large sprigs fresh dill, or 1½ tsp dill seed

salt

low-fat mayonnaise (optional)

≈ Boil the beetroot and potatoes in their skins with the carrots until tender. Refrigerate for 2–3 hours.

≈ Peel and chop the cooked vegetables, apples and onions, and chop the dill.

≈ Mix them all together, and season with salt, tossing a few times. Serve with low-fat mayonnaise.

NUTRITION FACTS	
Amount per Serving	
Calories 85	Calories from Fat 4
	% Daily Value
Total Fat 0.4g	0.6%
Saturated Fat 0.1g	0.5%
Polyunsaturated Fat 0.2g	0%
Monounsaturated Fat 0g	0%
Cholesterol 0mg	0%
Sodium 50mg	2%
Total Carbohydrate 19.5g	6.5%
Dietary Fibre 5g	20%
Sugars 13.5g	0%
Protein 2g	0%

Percent daily values are based on a 2000 calorie diet

AVOCADO AND POMEGRANATE SALAD

SERVES 4

Avocados are popular and are used in many salads and appetizer dishes. Oranges and pomegranates combine perfectly in this salad which makes an unusual first course or side dish for a main meal.

≈ In a small bowl, whisk together wine vinegar, orange juice, salt and pepper to taste, and honey. Slowly whisk in olive oil and vegetable oil until dressing is thick and creamy. Stir in the chopped mint. Set aside.

≈ Into a medium bowl, scrape seeds out of pomegranate halves. Add grape halves and toss to mix.

≈ Cut avocados in half and remove pits. Using a round-bladed knife, cut between skin and flesh of avocados, working skin away from flesh until skin is removed.

≈ Place avocados round-side up on work surface and, using a sharp knife and starting ½ in (2.5 cm) below stem end, cut each avocado lengthwise into ¼-in (¾-cm) slices, leaving stem end intact. Arrange sliced avocado halves on 4 individual plates. Using palm of hand, gently push avocado slices forward to fan out slices. Sprinkle lemon juice over them.

≈ Sprinkle a quarter of the pomegranate seed-grape mixture onto each avocado half and spoon over dressing. Garnish each plate with a few mint leaves.

1 ripe pomegranate, cut in half

8 oz (225 g) black grapes, cut in half and seeded

2 ripe avocados

1 tbsp lemon juice

Dressing

4 tbsp white-wine vinegar

2 tbsp orange juice

salt and freshly ground black pepper

1 tsp honey

1 tsp olive oil

1 tbsp peanut or sunflower oil

2 tbsp chopped fresh mint

Garnish

fresh mint leaves

NUTRITION FACTS	
Amount per Serving	
Calories 237	Calories from Fat 180
	% Daily Value
Total Fat 20g	31%
Saturated Fat 4g	20%
Polyunsaturated Fat 3g	0%
Monounsaturated Fat 12g	0%
Cholesterol 0mg	0%
Sodium 6mg	0.25%
Total Carbohydrate 13g	4%
Dietary Fibre 6g	24%
Sugars 12g	0%
Protein 2g	0%

Percent daily values are based on a 2000 calorie diet

STARFRUIT AND ROCKET SALAD WITH RASPBERRY DRESSING

SERVES 4

This makes a very good side salad or appetizer. Rocket has a strong, very distinctive flavour which is excellent when balanced with sweet salad greens such as iceberg or cos lettuce, but do not be tempted to add too much rocket or cut it too coarsely as it will overpower the other delicate ingredients, especially the starfruit. If rocket is not available a bunch or two of watercress may be used instead.

≈ Toss the lettuce, rocket and spring onions together in a salad bowl. Next make the dressing: place the vinegar in a basin and whisk in the sugar with plenty of seasoning. Continue whisking until the sugar and salt have dissolved. Slowly add the olive oil, whisking all the time to combine the ingredients well.

≈ Add the starfruit to the salad. Pour the dressing over and mix lightly. Serve at once. Do not leave the starfruit to stand for any length of time once it is cut since it dries on the surface and tends to discolour slightly around the edges.

½ iceberg lettuce, shredded

12 medium rocket leaves, finely shredded

3 spring onions, chopped

2 starfruit, sliced and quartered

Dressing

3 tbsp raspberry vinegar

1 tsp caster sugar

salt and freshly ground black pepper

8 tbsp olive oil

NUTRITION FACTS	
Amount per Serving	
Calories 237	Calories from Fat 200
	% Daily Value
Total Fat 22g	34%
Saturated Fat 3g	15%
Polyunsaturated Fat 2g	0%
Monounsaturated Fat 16g	0%
Cholesterol 0mg	0%
Sodium 4mg	0.2%
Total Carbohydrate 8g	3%
Dietary Fibre 1.5g	6%
Sugars 8g	0%
Protein 1g	0%

Percent daily values are based on a 2000 calorie diet

MEDITERRANEAN SALAD

SERVES 4

A ny combination of vegetables would be delicious steeped in this tomato and garlic sauce. Be sure to chill the dish well before serving and have crusty bread to hand to mop up the juices.

1¼ cups vegetable broth

1 onion, chopped fine

1 garlic clove, minced

¼ cup dry white wine

4 tomatoes, peeled and chopped

juice of 1 lime

1 tbsp cider vinegar

2 tsp tomato paste

1 tsp fennel seeds

1 tsp mustard seeds

1 cup button mushrooms, quartered

2 oz fine beans, trimmed

1 zucchini, sliced

ground black pepper

basil sprig to garnish

NUTRITION FACTS	
Serving Size 1 (311g)	
Calories 127	Calories from Fat 18
	% Daily Value
Total Fat 2g	3%
Saturated Fat 0g	1%
Monounsaturated Fat 0.3g	0%
Polyunsaturated Fat 0.4g	0%
Cholesterol 0mg	0%
Sodium 516mg	22%
Total Carbohydrate 23g	8%
Dietary Fiber 2g	8%
Sugars 6g	0%
Protein 6g	0%

Percent daily values are based on a 2000 calorie diet

≈ Heat the broth in a large saucepan and cook the onion and garlic for 3–4 minutes. Add the wine, tomatoes, lime juice, vinegar, tomato paste, fennel, and mustard seeds and the vegetables. Bring the mixture to a boil, reduce the heat and simmer for 20 minutes or until the vegetables are just cooked. Season with black pepper to taste.

≈ Transfer the mixture to a serving dish, cover and chill for at least 1 hour. Garnish with basil and serve.

SPINACH AND FIG SALAD

SERVES 4

450 g/1 lb fresh spinach, washed

25 g/1 oz pine nuts

3 fresh figs

4 tbsp lemon dressing

a few fresh nasturtium flowers
(optional)

≈ Remove and discard any coarse stems from the spinach and tear the leaves into pieces. Place in a colander to drain well. Place the pine nuts in a small, dry pan over medium-high heat, and roast until lightly browned, stirring all the time. Remove from the pan and leave to cool.

≈ Wash the figs, trim off the stems, cut each into quarters and then into thin slices. Place the spinach, pine nuts and figs in a serving bowl. Sprinkle the dressing over the mixture, toss well, and garnish with a few fresh nasturtium flowers, if available.

NUTRITION FACTS	
Amount per Serving	
Calories 81	Calories from Fat 36
	% Daily Value
Total Fat 4g	6%
Saturated Fat 0.4g	2%
Polyunsaturated Fat 2.5g	0%
Monounsaturated Fat 1g	0%
Cholesterol 0mg	0%
Sodium 160mg	7%
Total Carbohydrate 6g	2%
Dietary Fibre 4g	16%
Sugars 6g	0%
Protein 4g	0%

Percent daily values are based on a 2000 calorie diet

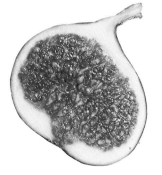

BAKED SALAD OF RED PEPPERS AND TOMATO

SERVES 4

The name of this recipe is asadilla, *meaning "little baked vegetables" and this all-red salad is a summer favourite. It can be served with lightly toasted bread or decorated with anchovy strips.*

2 large red peppers

2 beefsteak tomatoes

3 tbsp olive oil

2 garlic cloves, finely chopped

1 tbsp chopped fresh oregano

salt and freshly ground black pepper

≈ Skin the peppers. Hold them on a carving fork over a gas flame, until black and blistered. (Alternatively grill, giving them a quarter turn every 5 minutes.) Put them in a plastic bag for 10 minutes. Then strip off the skins. Pull out the stems and discard the seeds but reserve the juice.

≈ Meanwhile, skin the tomatoes, quarter them, remove seeds and juice (reserving it for later). Slice the tomato flesh lengthways into strips and put into an oiled baking dish.

≈ Slice the peppers the same way and mix in. Sprinkle with the garlic, herbs, remaining oil and salt and pepper. Press the tomato and pepper juices through a sieve, add them and mix everything gently. Bake in a preheated oven (at the highest temperature possible) for about 20 minutes then leave until cold.

≈ This is delicious as a salad, but it can also be puréed to make a sauce for other dishes. Because it stores well in a screw-top jar in the refrigerator (for a week or more), it is worth doubling and trebling quantities.

NUTRITION FACTS	
Amount per Serving	
Calories 117	Calories from Fat 80
	% Daily Value
Total Fat 9g	14%
Saturated Fat 1.5g	7.5%
Polyunsaturated Fat 1g	0%
Monounsaturated Fat 6g	0%
Cholesterol 0mg	0%
Sodium 10mg	0.4%
Total Carbohydrate 8g	3%
Dietary Fibre 3g	12%
Sugars 8g	0%
Protein 1.5g	0%

Percent daily values are based on a 2000 calorie diet

LIGHT LUNCHES AND SUPPERS

CURRIED LENTIL PÂTÉ

SERVES 8

Red lentils are used for speed in this recipe as they do not require pre-soaking. Should you wish to use other lentils, wash and soak them well and cook before using in the recipe.

3 cups vegetable broth

1 onion, chopped

3 garlic cloves, minced

1 tsp ground cumin

1 tsp ground coriander

½ tsp chili powder

1 scant cup red split lentils, washed

1 egg

4 tbsp skim milk

2 tbsp peach relish

2 tbsp fresh chopped cilantro

ground black pepper

cilantro sprigs to garnish

≈ Heat ⅔ cup of the vegetable broth in a saucepan and cook the onion and garlic for 2–3 minutes or until the onion begins to soften. Add the ground cumin, ground coriander, chili powder, lentils, and the remaining broth. Bring the mixture to a boil, then reduce the heat and simmer for 20 minutes or until the lentils are soft and cooked. Remove the pan from the heat and drain well.

≈ Transfer the mixture to a food processor and add the egg, milk, relish, chopped cilantro, and black pepper to taste. Blend for 10 seconds until smooth. Spoon into a non-stick 2 lb loaf pan and smooth the surface with the back of a spoon. Cover and cook in the oven at 400°F for 1 hour or until firm to the touch.

≈ Allow the pâté to cool before transferring to the refrigerator to chill. Unmold the pâté, slice, garnish with cilantro, and serve with a crisp salad.

ROASTED VEGETABLES ON TOAST

SERVES 4

The flavor of roasted vegetables is quite different from that achieved by boiling or steaming, and one not to be missed. This Mediterranean mixture is really colorful and tastes great with the light cheese sauce.

≈ Heat the oven to 400°F. Blanch all of the vegetables in boiling water for 8 minutes and drain well. Transfer the vegetables to a roasting pan and sprinkle the oil and rosemary over the top. Cook in the oven for 25 minutes or until softened and beginning to char slightly.

≈ Meanwhile, heat the broth for the sauce in a pan with the milk. Add the garlic, cream cheese, ground black pepper, and mustard. Blend the corn-starch with 2 tablespoons of cold water to form a paste and stir into the sauce. Bring to a boil, stirring until thickened and add the rosemary.

≈ Cook the bread under the broiler for 2–3 minutes each side until golden. Arrange two slices of the toast on four warmed serving plates and top with the roast vegetables. Spoon on the sauce, garnish with basil and rosemary, and serve.

NUTRITION FACTS	
Serving Size 1 (139g)	
Calories 107	Calories from Fat 9
	% Daily Value
Total Fat 1g	2%
Saturated Fat 0g	1%
Monounsaturated Fat 0.3g	0%
Polyunsaturated Fat 0.2g	0%
Cholesterol 27mg	9%
Sodium 414mg	17%
Total Carbohydrate 17g	6%
Dietary Fiber 7g	28%
Sugars 4g	0%
Protein 8g	0%

Percent daily values are based on a 2000 calorie diet

Roasted Vegetables on Toast

1 head of fennel, trimmed and
  quartered

2 open cap flat mushrooms, peeled
  and sliced

1 courgette, sliced

1 red pepper, seeded, halved, and
  sliced

1 red onion, cut into eight pieces

15 ml (1 tbsp) sunflower oil

2 rosemary sprigs

8 small slices of thick wholemeal
  bread

For the sauce

150 ml (¼ pint) vegetable stock

75 ml (3 fl oz) skimmed milk

2 garlic cloves, crushed

50 g (2 oz) low-fat cream cheese

ground black pepper

5 ml (1 tsp) Dijon mustard

15 g (1 tbsp) cornflour

1 rosemary sprig, chopped

basil and rosemary sprigs to garnish

NUTRITION FACTS	
Serving Size 1 (245g)	
Calories 250	Calories from Fat 72
	% Daily Value
Total Fat 8g	12%
Saturated Fat 1g	4%
Monounsaturated Fat 1.9g	0%
Polyunsaturated Fat 1.5g	0%
Cholesterol 9mg	3%
Sodium 430mg	18%
Total Carbohydrate 43g	14%
Dietary Fibre 7g	28%
Sugars 3g	0%
Protein 13g	0%

Per cent daily values are based on a 2000 calorie diet

SPINACH CRÊPES

SERVES 4

*These unusual light crêpes are made from a low-fat dough and rolled out.
Keep an eye on them during cooking as they can quickly brown.*

For the crêpes

75 g (3 oz) plain flour

125 ml (4 fl oz) water

5 ml (1 tsp) sunflower oil

For the filling

30 ml (2 tbsp) vegetable stock

1 small courgette, sliced

50 g (2 oz) spinach, shredded

1 small onion, chopped

65 g (2½ oz) button mushrooms, sliced

½ red pepper, seeded and cut into strips

1 celery stick, sliced

1 garlic clove, crushed

a pinch of ground nùtmeg

For the sauce

150 ml (¼ pint) skimmed milk

15 g (1 tbsp) cornflour

150 ml (¼ pint) vegetable stock

ground black pepper

15 g (1 tbsp) fresh chopped thyme

50 g (2 oz) low-fat vegetarian cheese, grated

2.5 g (½ tsp) paprika

≈ Sieve the flour for the crêpes into a mixing bowl and make a well in the centre. Heat the water and oil to boiling point and pour into the flour, mixing to form a dough. Turn on to a floured surface and knead for 3–4 minutes.

≈ Cut the mixture into four equal portions and roll each into a 15 cm (6 in) round. Heat a heavy, non-stick frying pan over medium heat. Put one of the crêpes into the pan and place another on top. Cook for 3–4 minutes, turning once when the bottom crêpe begins to brown. Cover the cooked crêpes with a clean, damp teatowel and repeat with remaining mixture. Cover and reserve.

≈ Heat the stock for the filling in a saucepan and cook the vegetables, garlic, and nutmeg for 7–8 minutes, stirring. Drain the mixture well.

≈ Blend 30 ml (2 tablespoons) of the milk for the sauce to a paste with the cornflour. Put in a saucepan with the remaining milk, vegetable stock, seasoning, thyme and half of the cheese. Bring the mixture to the boil, stirring until thickened.

≈ Heat the oven to 190°C (375°F, Gas 5). Spoon the vegetable mixture on to one half of each crêpe and roll up. Put in a shallow ovenproof dish, seam side down. Pour the sauce over the top and sprinkle with the remaining cheese and paprika. Cook in the oven for 15 minutes until golden brown. Serve immediately with salad.

NUTRITION FACTS	
Serving Size 1 (267g)	
Calories 174	Calories from Fat 27
	% Daily Value
Total Fat 3g	4%
Saturated Fat 0g	2%
Monounsaturated Fat 0.6g	0%
Polyunsaturated Fat 0.7g	0%
Cholesterol 1mg	0%
Sodium 390mg	16%
Total Carbohydrate 32g	11%
Dietary Fibre 2g	6%
Sugars 4g	0%
Protein 7g	0%

Per cent daily values are based on a 2000 calorie diet

PASTA CAPONATA

SERVES 4

Caponata is a well-known tomato and vegetable dish which is perfect to serve hot as a low-fat pasta sauce. In this recipe dried penne has been used but any pasta shapes or noodles would work equally well.

1 large aubergine

salt

150 ml (¼ pint) vegetable stock

1 onion, halved and sliced

2 garlic cloves, crushed

475 ml (16 fl oz) plum tomatoes, chopped

30 ml (2 tbsp) cider vinegar

4 celery sticks, chopped

50 g (2 oz) green beans, trimmed

25 g (1 oz) stoned green olives, halved

15 g (1 tbsp) fresh chopped basil

ground black pepper

225 g (8 oz) dried penne

basil sprigs to garnish

≈ Cut the aubergine into chunks and put in a colander. Sprinkle with salt and leave to stand for 20 minutes. Wash under cold water and pat dry. Cook the aubergine under a medium grill for 5 minutes, turning until browned.

≈ Meanwhile, heat the stock in a saucepan and add the onion and garlic. Cook for 2–3 minutes until softened. Stir in the tomatoes, vinegar, celery and beans. Cook over a gentle heat for 20 minutes, stirring occasionally. Add the aubergine, olives, and basil, season and cook for a further 10 minutes.

≈ Meanwhile, cook the penne in boiling salted water for 8–10 minutes or until just tender. Drain well and toss into the sauce. Spoon into a warmed serving dish, garnish with basil and serve.

NUTRITION FACTS	
Serving Size 1 (342g)	
Calories 324	Calories from Fat 27
	% Daily Value
Total Fat 3g	5%
Saturated Fat 0g	1%
Monounsaturated Fat 1.0g	0%
Polyunsaturated Fat 0.8g	0%
Cholesterol 0mg	0%
Sodium 333mg	14%
Total Carbohydrate 64g	21%
Dietary Fibre 5g	20%
Sugars 6g	0%
Protein 12g	0%

Per cent daily values are based on a 2000 calorie diet

CHESTNUT HASH

SERVES 4

675 g (1½ lb) potatoes, peeled and
    cubed

1 red onion, halved and sliced

75 g (3 oz) mangetout

50 g (2 oz) broccoli florets

1 courgette, sliced

1 green pepper, seeded and sliced

40 g (1½ oz) drained, canned corn

2 garlic cloves, crushed

5 g (1 tsp) paprika

30 g (2 tbsp) fresh chopped parsley

150 ml (¼ pint) vegetable stock

25 g (1 oz) chestnuts, cooked, peeled
    and quartered

ground black pepper

parsley sprigs to garnish

Cook the potatoes for this dish in advance or use up any leftover cooked potatoes for speed. Allow the potato to brown on the base of the pan for a crunchier texture.

≈ Cook the potatoes in boiling water for 20 minutes or until softened. Drain well and reserve.

≈ Meanwhile, cook the remaining ingredients in a frying pan for 10 minutes, stirring. Add the drained potatoes to the pan and cook for a further 15 minutes, stirring and pressing down with the back of a spoon. Serve immediately with crusty bread.

NUTRITION FACTS	
Serving Size 1 (396g)	
Calories 247	Calories from Fat 9
	% Daily Value
Total Fat 1g	2%
Saturated Fat 0g	1%
Monounsaturated Fat 0.2g	0%
Polyunsaturated Fat 0.3g	0%
Cholesterol 0mg	0%
Sodium 431mg	18%
Total Carbohydrate 55g	18%
Dietary Fibre 5g	22%
Sugars 8g	0%
Protein 7g	0%

Per cent daily values are based on a 2000 calorie diet

AUBERGINE-STUFFED MUSHROOMS

SERVES 4

Make the aubergine purée in advance for this recipe and store in the refrigerator for up to one day.

1 aubergine

2 garlic cloves, crushed

juice of 1 lime

1 cup wholemeal breadcrumbs

15 ml (1 tbsp) tomato purée

15 g (1 tbsp) fresh chopped
    coriander

8 large open cap mushrooms, peeled

25 g (1 oz) low-fat vegetarian
    cheese, grated

60 ml (4 tbsp) vegetable stock

coriander sprigs to garnish

≈ Heat the oven to 220°C (425°F, Gas 7). Cut the aubergine in half lengthways and place skin side uppermost in a baking dish. Cook in the oven for 30 minutes until soft. Remove the aubergine from the oven and allow to cool. Scoop the soft flesh from the skin and put in a food processor with the garlic and lime juice. Add the breadcrumbs to the food processor with the tomato purée and coriander and blend for 10 seconds to mix well.

≈ Spoon the purée on to the mushrooms pressing the mixture down. Sprinkle the cheese on top and transfer the mushrooms to a shallow ovenproof dish. Pour the stock around the mushrooms, cover and cook in the oven for 20 minutes. Remove the cover and cook for a further 5 minutes until golden on top.

≈ Remove the mushrooms from the oven and from the dish with a draining spoon. Serve with a mixed salad and garnish with coriander.

NUTRITION FACTS	
Serving Size 1 (128g)	
Calories 161	Calories from Fat 27
	% Daily Value
Total Fat 3g	5%
Saturated Fat 1g	3%
Monounsaturated Fat 1.4g	0%
Polyunsaturated Fat 0.7g	0%
Cholesterol 0mg	0%
Sodium 389mg	16%
Total Carbohydrate 27g	9%
Dietary Fibre 3g	12%
Sugars 1g	0%
Protein 6g	0%

Per cent daily values are based on a 2000 calorie diet

SPINACH AND CARROT MOUSSE

SERVES 8

This is an impressive dish which is deceiving as it is so simple. It is ideal for entertaining as it may be made in advance and chilled.

450 g (1 lb) spinach, stalks removed

5 g (1 tsp) ground ginger

5 g (1 tsp) curry powder

1 onion, chopped

425 g (15 oz) carrots, grated

2 garlic cloves, crushed

60 ml (4 tbsp) vegetable stock

4 egg whites

courgette strips to garnish

≈ Wash the spinach and cook, covered, in a large saucepan on a low heat for 5 minutes until wilted. Drain very well, squeezing out as much liquid as possible and blend in a food processor with the ginger and curry powder for 10 seconds. Transfer the purée to a mixing bowl.

≈ Cook the onion, carrots and garlic in the stock for 10 minutes or until the carrots are soft. Put in a food processor and liquidize for 10 seconds. Transfer to a separate mixing bowl.

≈ Whisk the egg whites until peaking and fold half into each of the vegetable purées. Spoon half of the carrot mixture into the base of a non-stick 900 g (2 lb) loaf tin, top with half of the spinach mixture and repeat once more. Cover and stand in a roasting tin half filled with boiling water.

≈ Heat the oven to 180°C (350°F, Gas 4). Cook the mousse for 1 hour or until set. Leave to cool and then transfer to the fridge to chill completely. Turn the mousse on to a serving plate, arrange courgette strips around the base and serve.

VEGETABLE CALZONE

SERVES 4

Calzone or pizza dough pasties are perfect for filling with your favourite ingredients. In this recipe the dough is slightly sweetened with honey for added flavour, but seeds or herbs could be added to the dough, or even garlic for variety.

≈ Sift the flour for the dough into a large mixing bowl. Add the yeast and make a well in the centre. Stir in the honey and stock and bring together to a dough. Turn the dough on to a lightly floured surface and knead for 10 minutes until smooth and elastic. Put in a mixing bowl, cover, and leave in a warm place to prove for 1 hour or until doubled in size.

≈ Meanwhile, heat the stock for the filling in a saucepan and stir in the tomatoes, basil, garlic, tomato purée, celery and leek and cook for 5 minutes, stirring.

≈ Divide the risen dough into four equal pieces. Roll each out on a lightly floured surface to a circle 18 cm (7 in) in diameter. Spoon equal amounts of the filling on to one half of each dough circle. Sprinkle with cheese. Brush the edge with milk and fold the dough over to form four semicircles. Crimp the seams, pressing together to seal and transfer the calzone to a non-stick baking sheet. Brush with milk.

≈ Heat the oven to 220°C (425°F, Gas 7). Cook the calzone for 30 minutes until risen and golden. Serve with salad.

NUTRITION FACTS	
Serving Size 1 (166g)	
Calories 49	Calories from Fat 9
	% Daily Value
Total Fat 1g	1%
Saturated Fat 0g	0%
Monounsaturated Fat 0.0g	0%
Polyunsaturated Fat 0.1g	0%
Cholesterol 0mg	0%
Sodium 208mg	9%
Total Carbohydrate 6g	2%
Dietary Fibre 3g	13%
Sugars 1g	0%
Protein 7g	0%

Per cent daily values are based on a 2000 calorie diet

Vegetable Calzone

For the dough

450 g (1 lb) white bread flour

5 g (1 tsp) easy-blend dried yeast

15 ml (1 tbsp) clear honey

300 ml (½ pint) vegetable stock

skimmed milk for glazing

For the filling

125 ml (4 fl oz) vegetable stock

40 g (1½ oz) sundried tomatoes,
    chopped

30 g (2 tbsp) fresh chopped basil

2 garlic cloves, crushed

30 ml (2 tbsp) tomato purée

1 celery stick, sliced

1 leek, sliced

25 g (1 oz) low-fat vegetarian
    cheese, grated

NUTRITION FACTS	
Serving Size 1 (332g)	
Calories 584	Calories from Fat 45
	% Daily Value
Total Fat 5g	8%
Saturated Fat 0g	2%
Monounsaturated Fat 0.4g	0%
Polyunsaturated Fat 0.5g	0%
Cholesterol 0mg	0%
Sodium 653mg	27%
Total Carbohydrate 114g	38%
Dietary Fibre 3g	13%
Sugars 9g	0%
Protein 25g	0%

Per cent daily values are based on a 2000 calorie diet

STUFFED LETTUCE LEAVES

SERVES 4

These small lettuce parcels are packed with a spicy vegetable and rice filling, then baked with a tomato sauce for a complete meal in itself. Make the filling and the sauce in advance and assemble the dish just before required. The recipe would also adequately serve eight as an appetizer, with only one parcel per person.

300 ml (½ pint) vegetable stock

1 red onion, chopped

2 garlic cloves, crushed

65 g (2½ oz) button mushrooms, chopped

50 g (2 oz) brown rice

50 g (2 oz) drained, canned corn

5 g (1 tsp) curry powder

8 large, firm lettuce leaves such as iceberg or Cos

For the sauce

475 ml (16 fl oz) passata

5 ml (1 tsp) light soya sauce

2.5 ml (½ tsp) chilli sauce

15 g (1 tbsp) fresh chopped basil

5 g (1 tsp) light brown sugar

ground black pepper

≈ Heat 75 ml (5 tablespoons) of the vegetable stock in a saucepan, add the onion and garlic and cook for 3–4 minutes until the onion begins to soften. Stir in the mushrooms, rice, corn, curry powder and remaining stock, bring to the boil, reduce the heat and simmer for 30–40 minutes until the rice is cooked and the liquid has been absorbed.

≈ Meanwhile, mix all of the sauce ingredients in a pan and bring to the boil. Reduce the heat, cover, and simmer for 10 minutes.

≈ Heat the oven to 180°C (350°F, Gas 4). Place the lettuce leaves on a chopping board and spoon equal quantities of the rice filling into the centre of each. Wrap the leaves around the filling and place seam side down in an ovenproof dish. Spoon the sauce over the top and cook in the oven for 10 minutes. Serve immediately.

BEAN AND ASPARAGUS FRY

SERVES 4

Fresh green beans and tender young asparagus are complemented in this recipe by a honey and lime-based sauce. Use any mixture of green beans that you have to hand for a quick and delicious dish.

≈ Top and tail the beans and cut into 2.5 cm (1 in) slices, if necessary. Mix the beans and asparagus together.

≈ Heat the stock in a large frying pan and add the vegetables, honey, lime juice, pepper, garlic, fennel seeds and mustard. Cook, stirring for 7–8 minutes until the vegetables are cooked but crisp. Stir in the cheese and parsley and serve immediately.

NUTRITION FACTS	
Serving Size 1 (288g)	
Calories 87	Calories from Fat 9
	% Daily Value
Total Fat 1g	1%
Saturated Fat 0g	0%
Monounsaturated Fat 0.1g	0%
Polyunsaturated Fat 0.2g	0%
Cholesterol 0mg	0%
Sodium 771mg	32%
Total Carbohydrate 19g	6%
Dietary Fibre 2g	6%
Sugars 6g	0%
Protein 3g	0%

Per cent daily values are based on a 2000 calorie diet

Bean and Asparagus Fry

225 g (8 oz) mixed fresh beans (e.g. green, wax, or French beans)

225 g (8 oz) young asparagus spears

75 g (3 oz) shelled broad beans

125 ml (4 fl oz) vegetable stock

30 ml (2 tbsp) clear honey

15 ml (1 tbsp) lime juice

ground black pepper

3 garlic cloves, crushed

5 g (1 tsp) fennel seeds

5 ml (1 tsp) Dijon mustard

25 g (1 oz) low-fat vegetarian cheese, grated

30 g (2 tbsp) fresh chopped parsley

NUTRITION FACTS	
Serving Size 1 (196g)	
Calories 295	Calories from Fat 27
	% Daily Value
Total Fat 3g	5%
Saturated Fat 0g	2%
Monounsaturated Fat 1.0g	0%
Polyunsaturated Fat 1.0g	0%
Cholesterol 0mg	0%
Sodium 509mg	21%
Total Carbohydrate 53g	18%
Dietary Fibre 10g	39%
Sugars 12g	0%
Protein 18g	0%

Per cent daily values are based on a 2000 calorie diet

GARLIC AUBERGINE ROLLS

SERVES 8

These may take a little preparation but they are well worth the effort. Cooking garlic in its skin takes away the strong flavour and produces a milder garlic purée. This can be cooked in advance with the aubergine and gently warmed through to make the rolls.

8 garlic cloves

1 aubergine, sliced

15 ml (1 tbsp) sunflower oil

25 g (1 oz) sundried tomatoes, reconstituted and sliced

30 g (2 tbsp) basil leaves, shredded

4 lettuce leaves, shredded

4 ciabatta or crusty large rolls

≈ Heat the oven to 200°C (400°F, Gas 6). Put the garlic and aubergine slices on a non-stick baking sheet and cook in the oven for 30 minutes until soft. Remove from the oven and cool.

≈ Squeeze the garlic purée from the cloves and reserve. Mix the tomatoes, basil and lettuce leaves together. Heat the rolls in a warm oven for 2–3 minutes and slice in half. Spread the garlic purée on to one half of each roll and top with the aubergine slices. Add the tomato mixture and top with remaining roll halves. Serve hot.

NUTRITION FACTS	
Serving Size 1 (83g)	
Calories 132	Calories from Fat 27
	% Daily Value
Total Fat 3g	5%
Saturated Fat 0g	2%
Monounsaturated Fat 1.3g	0%
Polyunsaturated Fat 0.2g	0%
Cholesterol 0mg	0%
Sodium 166mg	7%
Total Carbohydrate 23g	8%
Dietary Fibre 1g	5%
Sugars 0g	0%
Protein 4g	0%

Per cent daily values are based on a 2000 calorie diet

CHINESE NOODLES

SERVES 4

This is a really quick and easy dish for a speedy lunch or supper. Use egg or rice noodles for a Chinese flavour or pasta ribbons if preferred, but these will require cooking for 8–10 minutes.

225 g (8 oz) thin egg or rice noodles

75 ml (3 fl oz) vegetable stock

2 garlic cloves, crushed

1 red onion, halved and sliced

2.5 cm (1 in) piece of root ginger, grated

1 red chilli, chopped

2 carrots, cut into strips

50 g (2 oz) sugar snap peas

1 courgette, sliced

1 celery stick, sliced

5 g (1 tsp) curry powder

45 ml (3 tbsp) dark soya sauce

45 ml (3 tbsp) plum sauce

5 g (1 tsp) fennel seeds

fresh chopped parsley or fennel leaves to garnish

≈ Cook the noodles in boiling water for 3 minutes. Drain and reserve. Meanwhile, heat the stock in a non-stick wok or frying pan and cook the vegetables and spices for 3–4 minutes, stirring constantly.

≈ Add the drained noodles to the pan with the soya and plum sauces and the fennel seeds. Cook for 2–3 minutes, tossing well and serve garnished with parsley or fennel leaves.

NUTRITION FACTS	
Serving Size 1 (265g)	
Calories 139	Calories from Fat 9
	% Daily Value
Total Fat 1g	1%
Saturated Fat 0g	1%
Monounsaturated Fat 0.2g	0%
Polyunsaturated Fat 0.1g	0%
Cholesterol 0mg	0%
Sodium 1004mg	42%
Total Carbohydrate 31g	10%
Dietary Fibre 4g	14%
Sugars 9g	0%
Protein 4g	0%

Per cent daily values are based on a 2000 calorie diet

DIPS, SALSAS, RELISHES AND SAUCES

YOGURT, CUCUMBER AND GARLIC DIP

SERVES 4

450 ml/16 fl oz natural yogurt

½ cucumber

3 garlic cloves, crushed

2 tbsp chopped fresh mint

2 tbsp olive oil

1 tbsp white-wine vinegar

salt, to taste

Garnish

chopped fresh mint

This light and refreshing dip should always be served well chilled. It is very easy to make, and delicious on its own with fresh pitta bread or as an accompaniment to fritters and other fried foods.

≈ Place the yogurt in a medium-sized bowl. Peel and grate the cucumber, squeezing a little at a time in the palm of your hand to remove the excess water. Stir the cucumber into the yogurt.

≈ Stir in the garlic, fresh mint, olive oil and vinegar; season with salt, to taste. Cover and chill in the refrigerator until required. Just before serving, garnish with chopped fresh mint.

NUTRITION FACTS	
Amount per Serving	
Calories 125	Calories from Fat 60
	% Daily Value
Total Fat 6.5g	10%
Saturated Fat 1g	5%
Polyunsaturated Fat 0.5g	0%
Monounsaturated Fat 4g	0%
Cholesterol 5mg	2%
Sodium 96mg	4%
Total Carbohydrate 10g	3%
Dietary Fibre 1g	4%
Sugars 10g	0%
Protein 7g	0%

Percent daily values are based on a 2000 calorie diet

STARFRUIT AND BLACK BEAN SALSA

SERVES 6

This salsa is an unusual accompaniment for grilled dishes.

225 g/8-oz can black beans, drained

140 g/5 oz corn kernels, fresh, frozen, or canned and drained

225 g/8 oz ripe tomatoes, chopped

4 spring onions, trimmed and chopped

½ green pepper, seeded and finely diced

½ red pepper, seeded and finely diced

2 tbsp olive oil

110 ml/4 fl oz red-wine vinegar

chilli sauce to taste

ground cumin to taste

salt and freshly ground black pepper to taste

1 starfruit, ½ sliced crosswise in thin sections, ½ diced

≈ Mix the beans with the corn, tomatoes, onions, peppers, olive oil and vinegar; season to taste with the chilli sauce, Worcestershire sauce, cumin, and salt and pepper. Stir diced starfruit slices into the mixture and place the other slices across the top.

≈ Cover and refrigerate at least 3 hours to allow the flavours to blend, then serve chilled.

NUTRITION FACTS	
Amount per Serving	
Calories 128	Calories from Fat 45
	% Daily Value
Total Fat 5g	8%
Saturated Fat 1g	5%
Polyunsaturated Fat 1g	0%
Monounsaturated Fat 3g	0%
Cholesterol 0mg	0%
Sodium 110mg	5%
Total Carbohydrate 17g	6%
Dietary Fibre 4g	16%
Sugars 6g	0%
Protein 5g	0%

Percent daily values are based on a 2000 calorie diet

PINEAPPLE-COCONUT RELISH

SERVES 6

225 g/8 oz diced ripe pineapple

110 g/4 oz seeded and diced yellow
pepper

½ diced red onion

1 diced chilli pepper

110 g/4 oz unsweetened shredded
dry coconut

1 tbsp sherry vinegar

≈ Combine all ingredients in bowl.

≈ Cover and let stand at room
temperature for at least 10–15 minutes
until ready to serve.

NUTRITION FACTS	
Amount per Serving	
Calories 62	Calories from Fat 45
	% Daily Value
Total Fat 5g	8%
Saturated Fat 4.5g	22%
Polyunsaturated Fat 0.2g	0%
Monounsaturated Fat 0.3g	0%
Cholesterol 0mg	0%
Sodium 3mg	0.1%
Total Carbohydrate 3g	1%
Dietary Fibre 2g	8%
Sugars 3g	0%
Protein 1g	0%

Percent daily values are based on a 2000 calorie diet

GUACAMOLE

SERVES 4

When you make guacamole, make plenty: it is so delicious that a couple of mouthfuls is more tantalizing than satisfying. The recipe below is (just) enough for four; serve with corn chips.

≈ Seed and shred the chilli pepper; pound in a mortar with the garlic and 1–2 tbsp of water. Leave for 5–10 minutes. Mash the avocado with a potato masher. Mix in the chilli pepper-garlic paste, strained through a tea-strainer.

≈ This is good for a dip; for a garnish, you can double the amounts of garlic and pepper.

½ dried chilli pepper

1 clove garlic

2 large or 4 small avocados, very ripe

NUTRITION FACTS	
Amount per Serving	
Calories 138	Calories from Fat 126
	% Daily Value
Total Fat 14g	21%
Saturated Fat 3g	15%
Polyunsaturated Fat 2g	0%
Monounsaturated Fat 9g	0%
Cholesterol 0mg	0%
Sodium 4mg	0.2%
Total Carbohydrate 1.5g	0.5%
Dietary Fibre 4g	16%
Sugars 0.4g	0%
Protein 1g	0%

Percent daily values are based on a 2000 calorie diet

FANCY GUACAMOLE

SERVES 4

≈ Peel, seed, and finely chop the tomato. Chop the onion finely in a food processor. Add these ingredients to the guacamole. Salt if desired.

≈ For further variations, omit the red pepper or the garlic or both, and add one finely chopped serrano chilli. You may also wish to add chopped coriander. None of this will necessarily make a better guacamole, just a different one.

basic ingredients, as for guacamole

1 medium tomato

½ small onion

1 tbsp chopped coriander

salt

NUTRITION FACTS	
Amount per Serving	
Calories 146	Calories from Fat 126
	% Daily Value
Total Fat 14g	21.5%
Saturated Fat 3g	15%
Polyunsaturated Fat 2g	0%
Monounsaturated Fat 9g	0%
Cholesterol 0mg	0%
Sodium 7mg	0.3%
Total Carbohydrate 3g	1%
Dietary Fibre 4g	16%
Sugars 1.5g	0%
Protein 2g	0%

Percent daily values are based on a 2000 calorie diet

CURRY-LIME VINAIGRETTE

SERVES 6

A delicious complement to artichokes, mushrooms and asparagus, this vinaigrette substitutes refreshing lime for the usual lemon.

1½ tsp grated lime zest

50 ml/2 fl oz lime juice

4 tbsp curry powder

110 ml/4 fl oz safflower oil

salt and freshly ground black pepper
   to taste

paw-paw seeds to taste (optional)

≈ In a medium bowl, combine zest and lime juice. Whisk in curry powder, safflower oil and desired seasoning. Stir well and serve at room temperature.

NUTRITION FACTS

Amount per Serving

Calories 169	Calories from Fat 162

	% Daily Value
Total Fat 18g	28%
Saturated Fat 2g	10%
Polyunsaturated Fat 13g	0%
Monounsaturated Fat 2g	0%
Cholesterol 0mg	0%
Sodium 10mg	0.4%
Total Carbohydrate 1g	0.3%
Dietary Fibre 1g	4%
Sugars 0.1g	0%
Protein 0.2g	0%

Percent daily values are based on a 2000 calorie diet

PEPPER-LIME DIP

SERVES 6

This dip complements many vegetable dishes but is especially good with artichokes.

½ tsp salt

1 clove garlic, minced

1 small chilli pepper, seeded and
   minced

50 ml/2 fl oz lime juice

100 ml/3 fl oz minced onion

6 tbsp cold water

1–2 tbsp chopped fresh coriander
   (optional)

≈ Mash salt with garlic and chilli pepper to form a paste. Stir in lime juice, onion, water and coriander, if desired.

≈ Let stand 1 hour before serving.

NUTRITION FACTS

Amount per Serving

Calories 5	Calories from Fat 0

	% Daily Value
Total Fat 0g	0%
Saturated Fat 0g	0%
Polyunsaturated Fat 0g	0%
Monounsaturated Fat 0g	0%
Cholesterol 0mg	0%
Sodium 1mg	0%
Total Carbohydrate 1g	0.3%
Dietary Fibre 0.2g	0.8%
Sugars 1g	0%
Protein 0.2g	0%

Percent daily values are based on a 2000 calorie diet

SAVOURY KUMQUAT SAUCE

MAKES 550 ML/1 PT

This is a savoury, orange-type sauce to serve with all kinds of vegetable dishes.

2 spring onions, trimmed and sliced

1 tsp freshly grated ginger

peel of 1 lime, thinly cut into strips

110 g/4 oz kumquats, cut into
  quarters with seeds removed

½ vegetable bouillon cube

550 ml/1 pt water

finely grated peel and juice of
  1 orange

3 tbsp cornflour

2 tbsp sugar

NUTRITION FACTS	
Amount per Serving (550 ml)	
Calories 429	Calories from Fat 9
	% Daily Value
Total Fat 1g	1.5%
Saturated Fat 0.1g	0.5%
Polyunsaturated Fat 0.2g	0%
Monounsaturated Fat 0.1g	0%
Cholesterol 0mg	0%
Sodium 41mg	2%
Total Carbohydrate 110g	37%
Dietary Fibre 5g	20%
Sugars 55g	0%
Protein 2g	0%

Percent daily values are based on a 2000 calorie diet

≈ Put the onions, ginger, lime, kumquats, bouillon cube and water into a saucepan and cook for about 10–15 minutes until the kumquats are soft.

≈ Blend the orange juice and peel with the cornflour and stir into the kumquat mixture. Bring slowly to a boil, stirring, and cook for 2–3 minutes until thickened and clear. Add sugar to taste.

PAW-PAW-MANGO SALSA

SERVES 6

≈ Peel, seed the paw-paw and mango, and cut into bite-sized pieces. Seed and mince the jalapeño pepper.

≈ In a medium bowl, combine with all the remaining ingredients, cover and refrigerate. Serve chilled.

½ paw-paw

½ mango

1 fresh jalapeño pepper

1 spring onion, chopped

1 tbsp sugar

1 tbsp chopped fresh coriander

1 tbsp finely chopped red pepper

paw-paw seeds to taste (optional)

NUTRITION FACTS	
Amount per Serving	
Calories 29	Calories from Fat 0
	% Daily Value
Total Fat 0g	0%
Saturated Fat 0g	0%
Polyunsaturated Fat 0g	0%
Monounsaturated Fat 0g	0%
Cholesterol 0mg	0%
Sodium 8mg	0.3%
Total Carbohydrate 7g	2%
Dietary Fibre 2g	8%
Sugars 5g	0%
Protein 0.3g	0%

Percent daily values are based on a 2000 calorie diet

MANGO AND GREEN TOMATO CHUTNEY

MAKES APPROXIMATELY 1.8 KG/4 LB

900 g/2 lb mangoes, peeled and
    quartered
675 mg/1½ lb tart apples, peeled and
    chopped
1 onion, chopped
450 g/1 lb green tomatoes, chopped
160 g/6 oz raisins
juice of 1 large lemon
560 ml/1 pt vinegar
2 tbsp salt
¼ tsp cayenne pepper
¼ tsp nutmeg
3 bay leaves
1½ tbsp lime juice
900 g/2 lb brown sugar

≈ Place all the ingredients except the lime juice and sugar in a large bowl, mix thoroughly and leave to stand for at least 3 hours.

≈ Transfer to a preserving pan, bring to the boil and simmer gently until tender, stirring frequently.

≈ Add the lime juice and sugar and stir until the sugar is dissolved. Continue to simmer until thick and of the desired consistency.

≈ Pour into warmed jars, cover and label.

NUTRITION FACTS	
Amount (makes approx. 1.8 kg)	
Calories 4348	Calories from Fat 40
	% Daily Value
Total Fat 4.5g	7%
Saturated Fat 1g	5%
Polyunsaturated Fat 2g	0%
Monounsaturated Fat 0.5g	0%
Cholesterol 0mg	0%
Sodium 640mg	27%
Total Carbohydrate 1140g	38%
Dietary Fibre 58g	232%
Sugars 1086g	0%
Protein 16g	0%

Percent daily values are based on a 2000 calorie diet

PAW-PAW AND ORANGE RELISH

MAKES APPROXIMATELY 900 G/2 LB

≈ Place the onions, garlic, cider vinegar and ginger in a saucepan and cook for 10 minutes to slightly soften the onion.

≈ Halve the paw-paw, scoop out the seeds, and peel. Cut the flesh into small dice, and add to the remaining ingredients in the pan.

≈ Cook for about 15 minutes until the paw-paw is just cooked and still retains its shape. Remove the orange peel and whole spices, if desired. Remove the ginger and chilli peppers unless a hot relish is preferred. Pot into jars while still hot.

2 onions, chopped

3 small cloves garlic, crushed

225 ml/½ pt cider vinegar

4 cm/1½ in fresh ginger, sliced

2 medium-sized paw-paw (approx 675 g/1½ lb)

peel and juice of 1 orange

6 cloves garlic

3 dried chilli peppers

6 allspice berries

½ tsp salt

75 g/3 oz light soft brown sugar

110 g/4 oz seeded raisins, chopped

NUTRITION FACTS	
Amount per Serving (900 g)	
Calories 784	Calories from Fat 18
	% Daily Value
Total Fat 2g	3%
Saturated Fat 0.2g	1%
Polyunsaturated Fat 0.2g	0%
Monounsaturated Fat 0g	0%
Cholesterol 0mg	0%
Sodium 115mg	5%
Total Carbohydrate 188g	63%
Dietary Fibre 22g	88%
Sugars 182g	0%
Protein 8.5g	0%

Percent daily values are based on a 2000 calorie diet

dash each of salt and freshly ground
    black pepper

1 tsp sugar

½ tsp Dijon mustard

2 tbsp light oil

1 tbsp tarragon vinegar

3 tbsp low fat mayonnaise

2 tsp chopped fresh tarragon

350 g/12 oz strawberries, sliced

1 kiwi fruit, peeled and quartered

NUTRITION FACTS	
Amount per Serving (280 ml)	
Calories 534	Calories from Fat 400
	% Daily Value
Total Fat 44g	68%
Saturated Fat 3g	15%
Polyunsaturated Fat 14g	0%
Monounsaturated Fat 5g	0%
Cholesterol 17mg	6%
Sodium 780mg	32%
Total Carbohydrate 32g	11%
Dietary Fibre 5g	20%
Sugars 29g	0%
Protein 3g	0%

Percent daily values are based on a 2000 calorie diet

STRAWBERRY AND KIWI FRUIT RELISH

MAKES 280 ML/½ PT

This recipe could be made with low-fat yogurt instead of low-fat mayonnaise, depending on the accompanying dishes and personal preference. Serve chilled.

≈ Place the seasoning, sugar and mustard in a bowl, stir in the oil and gradually beat in the vinegar, mayonnaise and tarragon. Add the strawberries and the kiwi fruit. Chill and serve.

BANANA RELISH

MAKES 170 ML/6 FL OZ

Serve this relish with barbecued food.

≈ Melt the oil and fry the onion slowly, without browning, until soft. Stir in the mustard and sugar and cook for 1 minute.

≈ Mash the bananas and add the remaining ingredients. Cook for 2–3 minutes to soften the banana. Serve at room temperature.

1 tbsp olive oil

1 small onion, finely chopped

2 tsp grainy mustard

1 tsp sugar

4 medium-sized bananas, peeled

2 tsp white malt-vinegar

NUTRITION FACTS	
Amount per Serving (170 ml)	
Calories 588	Calories from Fat 110
	% Daily Value
Total Fat 12.5g	19%
Saturated Fat 2g	10%
Polyunsaturated Fat 1g	0%
Monounsaturated Fat 8g	0%
Cholesterol 0mg	0%
Sodium 126mg	5%
Total Carbohydrate 120g	40%
Dietary Fibre 7g	28%
Sugars 109g	0%
Protein 6g	0%

Percent daily values are based on a 2000 calorie diet

LEMON FENNEL SAUCE

MAKES 300 ML/½ PT

This is a sharp, tangy pouring sauce.

3 tbsp olive oil

1 bulb fresh fennel, finely chopped

2 tsp flour

grated peel of 1 lemon

juice of 2 lemons

150 ml/5 fl oz water

1 tbsp fresh fennel leaves, chopped

1 tsp sugar

salt and freshly ground black pepper

NUTRITION FACTS

Amount per Serving (300 ml)	
Calories 485	Calories from Fat 306

	% Daily Value
Total Fat 34g	52%
Saturated Fat 5g	25%
Polyunsaturated Fat 3g	0%
Monounsaturated Fat 24g	0%
Cholesterol 0mg	0%
Sodium 26mg	1%
Total Carbohydrate 42g	14%
Dietary Fibre 9g	36%
Sugars 11g	0%
Protein 6g	0%

Percent daily values are based on a 2000 calorie diet

≈ Heat the oil in a saucepan, add the chopped fennel and stir. Cover and cook gently for 5 minutes to soften.

≈ Add the flour and cook for 30 seconds, then stir in the lemon peel and juice, together with the water. Bring to the boil and cook for a further 2 minutes until thickened. Add the fennel leaves and sugar, if required. Season to taste.

PLUM AND RED WINE SAUCE

SERVES 4

Serve this sauce with ice cream or cheesecake.

225 g/½ lb red plums

230 ml/8 fl oz plus 2 tbsp water

115 g/4 oz sugar

125 ml/4 fl oz red wine

2 tsp arrowroot

2 tbsp water

≈ Wash the plums, halve them and remove the stones. Place the plums, water and sugar in a saucepan, heat and stir to dissolve the sugar. Add the wine and cook until the plums are soft. Purée the plums in a blender and return to the saucepan.

≈ Blend the arrowroot with 2 tbsp water and stir into the purée. Bring to the boil, stirring, until thickened and clear. If the sauce appears too thick, add a little extra water or orange juice.

NUTRITION FACTS	
Amount per Serving	
Calories 261	Calories from Fat 0
	% Daily Value
Total Fat 0g	0%
Saturated Fat 0g	0%
Polyunsaturated Fat 0g	0%
Monounsaturated Fat 0g	0%
Cholesterol 0mg	0%
Sodium 6mg	0.3%
Total Carbohydrate 64g	21%
Dietary Fibre 1g	4%
Sugars 61g	0%
Protein 0.5g	0%

Percent daily values are based on a 2000 calorie diet

ONION PURÉE

MAKES ABOUT 450 G/1 LB

This gently stewed mixture of onions and oil is the basis of many Mediterranean dishes and sauces. It can be made in advance and stored for several days in the refrigerator.

≈ Heat the oil in a heavy pan that has a lid. Stir in the onions, add salt, cover, and cook over a very low heat for about 1 hour, until the onions have softened and almost disintegrated.

≈ Add the garlic cloves, stir and increase the heat slightly. Leave to cook until the onions are an even brown. Remove the garlic, if preferred, and season to taste.

4 tsp olive oil

675 g/1½ lb onions, finely chopped

salt and pepper

3 garlic cloves

NUTRITION FACTS

Amount per Serving (450 g)

Calories 324　　　Calories from Fat 145

	% Daily Value
Total Fat 16g	25%
Saturated Fat 2g	10%
Polyunsaturated Fat 2g	0%
Monounsaturated Fat 11g	0%
Cholesterol 0mg	0%
Sodium 15mg	0.6%
Total Carbohydrate 41g	14%
Dietary Fibre 1.5g	6%
Sugars 28g	0%
Protein 7g	0%

Percent daily values are based on a 2000 calorie diet

RED PEPPER PASTE

MAKES ABOUT 300 ML/½ PT

A paste of roasted red peppers has now become a fashionable ingredient, but it has been used in the Mediterranean countries for many years as a flavouring for grills and marinades. The garlic cloves can also be roasted, before peeling, if liked. The paste can be kept in a covered glass jar in the refrigerator for 2 weeks.

≈ Stir together the peppers and salt; then leave, uncovered, at room temperature for 24 hours.
≈ Preheat the grill. Rinse the peppers well, drain and pat dry. Place, skin side up, on a baking sheet. Grill until the skins are charred and blistered. Leave to cool slightly before peeling off the skins and discarding.

≈ Purée the garlic and peppers in a blender, pouring in the oil slowly.

3 large red peppers, seeded and
　　quartered lengthwise

1 tbsp sea salt

2 garlic cloves

4 tbsp olive oil

NUTRITION FACTS

Amount per Serving (300 ml)

Calories 574　　　Calories from Fat 415

	% Daily Value
Total Fat 46g	71%
Saturated Fat 7g	35%
Polyunsaturated Fat 5g	0%
Monounsaturated Fat 32g	0%
Cholesterol 0mg	0%
Sodium 22mg	1%
Total Carbohydrate 36g	12%
Dietary Fibre 12g	48%
Sugars 33g	0%
Protein 6g	0%

Percent daily values are based on a 2000 calorie diet

PIRI-PIRI CHILLI SAUCE

MAKES ABOUT 5 TBSP

½ small red pepper

4–5 fresh red chilli peppers

juice of 1½ lemons

2 tsp olive oil

salt

NUTRITION FACTS	
Amount per Serving (1 tbsp)	
Calories 24	Calories from Fat 13
	% Daily Value
Total Fat 1.5g	2%
Saturated Fat 0.2g	1%
Polyunsaturated Fat 0.2g	0%
Monounsaturated Fat 1g	0%
Cholesterol 0mg	0%
Sodium 2mg	0%
Total Carbohydrate 2g	0.6%
Dietary Fibre 1g	4%
Sugars 2g	0%
Protein 0.4g	0%

Percent daily values are based on a 2000 calorie diet

This is a chilli-based sauce that provides the fire in many savoury dishes – it is easier to add a few drops of the ready-made chilli-based sauce than to seed and chop chilli peppers each time. Like other traditional recipes, nearly everyone who makes Piri-piri has their own version, the simplest of which is to fill a third of a jar or bottle with small, red chilli peppers, then top up with olive oil, cover and leave in a cool place for at least 1 month so the oil is impregnated with their heat. Other versions, like the one below, include lemon juice or vinegar. Hot pepper sauce can be substituted.

≈ De-seed and slice the pepper and red chilli peppers.

≈ Simmer the red pepper and chilli peppers in a saucepan with the lemon juice for about 15 minutes until tender.

≈ Place in a blender with the oil and mix until thick. Season with salt. Pour into a small bottle or jar, cover and keep in a cool place.

TOMATO SAUCE

MAKES ABOUT 600 ML/1 PT

6 tbsp olive oil

2 onions, chopped

1–2 garlic cloves, chopped

2 red peppers

1 fresh red chilli pepper

1 kg/2¼ lb tomatoes, chopped

salt and pepper

NUTRITION FACTS	
Amount per Serving (600 ml)	
Calories 929	Calories from Fat 640
	% Daily Value
Total Fat 71g	109%
Saturated Fat 11g	55%
Polyunsaturated Fat 8g	0%
Monounsaturated Fat 49g	0%
Cholesterol 0mg	0%
Sodium 110mg	4.5%
Total Carbohydrate 65g	22%
Dietary Fibre 25g	100%
Sugars 60g	0%
Protein 13g	0%

Percent daily values are based on a 2000 calorie diet

Tomato sauce is a staple for Mediterranean cooks. The special taste is not only because the tomatoes from this region are sweet and richly flavoured, but because of the amount of oil that is used, so do not reduce the quantity; it emulsifies with the other ingredients when the sauce is boiled or puréed. For a greater depth of tomato flavour, add a few pieces of sun-dried tomatoes, or a little sun-dried tomato paste.

≈ De-seed and slice the pepper and chilli pepper.

≈ Heat the oil, add the onion and garlic, and cook gently until they begin to soften. Stir in the peppers and chilli pepper and cook for a few minutes; then add the tomatoes and simmer, stirring occasionally, until reduced to the consistency of a sauce.

≈ Purée in a blender or food processor; then strain through a sieve to remove pieces of skin and the seeds. Season and reheat as required.

PLUM AND PUMPKIN RELISH

MAKES APPROXIMATELY 2.5 KG/5½ LB

This is a sweet and sour relish ideal for cheese. The pumpkin and onion should be slightly crisp.

900 g/2 lb piece of pumpkin

450 g/1 lb onions, sliced

300 ml/½ pt cider vinegar

6 cloves garlic, crushed

900 g/2 lb plums, halved and pitted

3 bay leaves

15 g/½ oz salt

85 g/3 oz seedless golden raisins

1 tbsp mustard seed

≈ Cut the flesh from the skin of the pumpkin and dice. Place in a large saucepan with the onions, cider vinegar and garlic. Cook slowly to just soften the pumpkin so it remains a bit crisp – about 20 minutes.

≈ Add the plums and bay leaves. Cook for a further 10–15 minutes to soften the plums without losing their shape.

≈ Remove the bay leaves. Stir in the remaining ingredients. Place in a large bowl, cover and leave for 1 week to allow the flavours to develop and the mustard seeds to swell. Stir from time to time.

≈ Store in jars.

NUTRITION FACTS	
Amount per Serving (2.5 kg)	
Calories 931	Calories from Fat 36
	% Daily Value
Total Fat 4g	6%
Saturated Fat 1g	5%
Polyunsaturated Fat 0.5g	0%
Monounsaturated Fat 0g	0%
Cholesterol 0mg	0%
Sodium 100mg	4%
Total Carbohydrate 200g	66%
Dietary Fibre 45g	180%
Sugars 182g	0%
Protein 22g	0%

Percent daily values are based on a 2000 calorie diet

MAIN DISHES

VEGETABLE LASAGNE

SERVES 4

This is a low fat version of a classic dish using a colourful mixture of vegetables to replace the meat. Serve with salad for a delicious combination.

1 small aubergine

salt

450 g (16 oz) can chopped tomatoes

2 garlic cloves, crushed

15 g (1 tbsp) chopped basil

1 large courgette, seeded and
  chopped

1 onion, chopped

1 green pepper, seeded and chopped

65 g (2½ oz) button mushrooms,
  sliced

5 g (1 tsp) chilli powder

ground black pepper

115 g (4 oz) lasagne verdi (no
  pre-cook variety)

For the sauce

150 ml (¼ pint) vegetable stock

300 ml (½ pint) skimmed milk

50 g (2 oz) low fat vegetarian
  cheese, grated

5 ml (1 tsp) Dijon mustard

30 g (2 tbsp) cornflour

15 g (1 tbsp) fresh chopped basil

≈ Slice the aubergine and put in a colander. Sprinkle with salt and leave for 30 minutes. Wash and pat dry.

≈ Put the tomatoes, garlic, basil, courgette, onion, pepper, mushrooms and chilli powder in a saucepan. Add the aubergine and cook for 30 minutes, stirring occasionally until the vegetables are cooked.

≈ Mix the stock for the sauce, the milk, half of the cheese and the mustard in a saucepan. Blend the cornflour with

. 60 ml (4 tablespoons) cold water to form a paste and add to the pan. Bring to the boil, stirring until thickened.

. ≈ Spoon a layer of the vegetable mixture into the base of an ovenproof dish. Lay half of the lasagne on top to cover. Spoon on remaining vegetable mixture and cover with the remaining lasagne. Pour the cheese sauce over the top and cook at 190°C (375°F, Gas 5) for 40 minutes or until golden and bubbling. Sprinkle the basil on top and serve.

VEGETABLE AND TOFU PIE

SERVES 8

In this recipe, firm tofu (bean curd) is cubed and added to the pie. If liked, use a marinated tofu for extra flavour and use in the same way.

≈ Place all of the vegetables and the tofu in a non-stick frying pan and dry fry for 3–5 minutes, stirring. Add the stock and coriander, season and cook for 20 minutes or until the vegetables are tender. Blend the cornflour to a paste with 30 ml (2 tablespoons) of cold water, add to the mixture and bring the mixture to the boil, stirring until thickened.

≈ Spoon the mixture into an ovenproof pie dish. Lay one sheet of filo pastry on top and brush with melted fat. Cut the remaining pastry into strips and lay on top, folding as you go to create a rippled effect. Sprinkle the remaining fat on top and cook the pie in the oven at 200°C (400°F, Gas 6) for 20 minutes until golden brown. Serve with new potatoes.

NUTRITION FACTS	
Serving Size 1 (401g)	
Calories 264	Calories from Fat 45
	% Daily Value
Total Fat 5g	7%
Saturated Fat 0g	2%
Monounsaturated Fat 1.7g	0%
Polyunsaturated Fat 0.9g	0%
Cholesterol 1mg	0%
Sodium 306mg	13%
Total Carbohydrate 45g	15%
Dietary Fibre 5g	19%
Sugars 10g	0%
Protein 13g	0%

Per cent daily values are based on a 2000 calorie diet

4 sheets of filo pastry

15 ml (1 tbsp) polyunsaturated
    low-fat spread, melted

For the filling

1 leek, sliced

2 garlic cloves, crushed

2 carrots, diced

115 g (4 oz) cauliflower florets

115 g (4 oz) French beans, halved

2 celery sticks, sliced

225 g (8 oz) firm tofu, diced

300 ml (½ pint) vegetable stock

30 g (2 tbsp) fresh chopped
    coriander

ground black pepper

15 g (1 tbsp) cornflour

Vegetable and Tofu Pie

NUTRITION FACTS	
Serving Size 1 (152g)	
Calories 130	Calories from Fat 27
	% Daily Value
Total Fat 3g	4%
Saturated Fat 0g	2%
Monounsaturated Fat 0.6g	0%
Polyunsaturated Fat 1.3g	0%
Cholesterol 0mg	0%
Sodium 257mg	11%
Total Carbohydrate 21g	7%
Dietary Fibre 1g	5%
Sugars 3g	0%
Protein 7g	0%

Per cent daily values are based on a 2000 calorie diet

MIXED BEAN CHILLI

SERVES 4

Chilli con carne has always been a warming favourite, and this recipe without the "carne" is no exception. Packed with vegetables and beans, it is a fully satisfying meal.

450 g (16 oz) canned beans such as
    borlotti, red kidney, black-eyed
    and pinto beans, drained

400 g (14 oz) can chopped tomatoes

15 ml (1 tbsp) tomato purée

1 onion, halved and sliced

150 g (5 oz) potatoes, cubed

1 green pepper, seeded and chopped

150 g (5 oz) baby corn, halved

2 green chillies, seeded and chopped

5 g (1 tsp) chilli powder

2 garlic cloves, crushed

150 ml (¼ pint) vegetable stock

fresh chopped parsley to garnish

NUTRITION FACTS	
Serving Size 1 (351g)	
Calories 178	Calories from Fat 9
	% Daily Value
Total Fat 1g	2%
Saturated Fat 0g	1%
Monounsaturated Fat 0.2g	0%
Polyunsaturated Fat 0.3g	0%
Cholesterol 0mg	0%
Sodium 808mg	34%
Total Carbohydrate 36g	12%
Dietary Fibre 7g	30%
Sugars 5g	0%
Protein 8g	0%

Per cent daily values are based on a 2000 calorie diet

≈ Place all of the ingredients except the garnish in a large saucepan and bring to the boil. Reduce the heat, cover the pan and simmer for 45 minutes or until all of the vegetables are cooked and the juices have thickened slightly. Stir the chilli occasionally while cooking.

≈ Garnish with parsley and serve with brown rice or baked potatoes.

VEGETABLE FLAN

SERVES 4

This flan is made with a low-fat pastry which is flavoured with mustard. Although it is not quite as short as a traditional pastry it is delicious hot when filled with vegetables and low-fat cheese.

For the pastry

115 g (4 oz) flour

30 ml (2 tbsp) skimmed milk

75 g (1½ tsp) baking powder

5 g (1 tsp) mustard powder

For the filling

1 celery stick, sliced

50 g (2 oz) button mushrooms, sliced

2 baby corn cobs, sliced

1 leek, sliced

2 garlic cloves, crushed

8 asparagus spears, trimmed

125 ml (4 fl oz) vegetable stock

115 g (4 oz) low-fat cottage cheese

150 ml (¼ pint) skimmed milk

1 egg white, beaten

≈ Heat the oven to 200°C (400°F, Gas 6). Mix the pastry ingredients in a bowl and add enough cold water to bring the mixture together to form a soft dough. Roll the pastry out on a lightly floured surface to fit an 20 cm (8 in) pie dish.

≈ Cook the prepared vegetables in the stock for 5 minutes, stirring. Remove from the pan with a draining spoon and place in a bowl. Add the cottage cheese, milk and egg white. Spoon the mixture into the pastry case and cook for 40 minutes until set and golden brown. Serve hot with salad.

NUTRITION FACTS	
Serving Size 1 (256g)	
Calories 207	Calories from Fat 18
	% Daily Value
Total Fat 2g	3%
Saturated Fat 0g	2%
Monounsaturated Fat 0.2g	0%
Polyunsaturated Fat 0.3g	0%
Cholesterol 2mg	1%
Sodium 506mg	21%
Total Carbohydrate 37g	12%
Dietary Fibre 2g	7%
Sugars 6g	0%
Protein 12g	0%

Per cent daily values are based on a 2000 calorie diet

STUFFED PASTA SHELLS

SERVES 4

These large pasta shells are ideal for filling and serving with a sauce. Quick to cook, they look fabulous and are great for entertaining.

16 large pasta shells

For the sauce

450 g (16 oz) can chopped tomatoes

2 garlic cloves, crushed

15 ml (1 tbsp) fresh chopped parsley

1 onion, chopped

2 tbsp tomato purée

ground black pepper

For the filling

60 ml (4 tbsp) vegetable stock

1 courgette, diced

40 g (1½ oz) canned or frozen corn kernels

1 green pepper, seeded and diced

50 g (2 oz) button mushrooms, sliced

1 leek, sliced

2 garlic cloves, crushed

15 g (1 tbsp) fresh chopped mixed herbs

basil sprigs to garnish

≈ Place the sauce ingredients in a pan, bring to the boil, cover, and simmer for 10 minutes. Transfer to a food processor and blend for 10 seconds. Return the sauce to the pan and heat through.

≈ Meanwhile, put all of the filling ingredients, except the herbs, in a saucepan and cook for 10 minutes, simmering until the vegetables are tender. Stir in the herbs and season.

≈ Cook the pasta in boiling salted water for 8–10 minutes until just tender, drain well. Spoon the vegetable filling into the pasta shells and arrange on warmed serving plates. Spoon the sauce around the shells, garnish with basil and serve.

WILD RICE AND LENTIL CASSEROLE

SERVES 4

This dish is superb on a cold day as it is really hearty and warming. To check that the rice is cooked, look at the ends to be sure they have split open, otherwise cook for a little longer until it is visibly cooked through.

≈ Cook the lentils and wild rice in the vegetable stock in a large flameproof casserole dish for 20 minutes, stirring occasionally.

≈ Add the onion, garlic, tomatoes, spices, mushrooms, pepper, broccoli and corn. Bring the mixture to the boil, reduce the heat and cook for a further 15 minutes until the rice and lentils are cooked. Add the chopped coriander, garnish and serve with warm crusty bread.

NUTRITION FACTS	
Serving Size 1 (251g)	
Calories 82	Calories from Fat 9
	% Daily Value
Total Fat 1g	2%
Saturated Fat 0g	1%
Monounsaturated Fat 0.19g	0%
Polyunsaturated Fat 0.3g	0%
Cholesterol 0mg	0%
Sodium 461mg	19%
Total Carbohydrate 18g	6%
Dietary Fibre 3g	13%
Sugars 7g	0%
Protein 3g	0%

Per cent daily values are based on a 2000 calorie diet

200 g (7 oz) red split lentils

50 g (2 oz) wild rice

1 litre (1¾ pints) vegetable stock

1 red onion, cut into eight pieces

2 garlic cloves, crushed

400 g (14 oz) can chopped tomatoes

5 g (1 tsp) ground coriander

5 g (1 tsp) ground cumin

5 g (1 tsp) chilli powder

salt and ground black pepper

200 g (7 oz) button mushrooms,
   sliced

1 green pepper, seeded and sliced

75 g (3 oz) broccoli florets

150 g (5 oz) baby corn cobs, halved

15 g (1 tbsp) fresh chopped
   coriander

coriander sprigs to garnish

Wild Rice and Lentil Casserole

NUTRITION FACTS	
Serving Size 1 (593g)	
Calories 242	Calories from Fat 27
	% Daily Value
Total Fat 3g	4%
Saturated Fat 0g	1%
Monounsaturated Fat 0.2g	0%
Polyunsaturated Fat 0.5g	0%
Cholesterol 0mg	0%
Sodium 1384mg	58%
Total Carbohydrate 43g	14%
Dietary Fibre 16g	66%
Sugars 7g	0%
Protein 18g	0%

Per cent daily values are based on a 2000 calorie diet

SPICY CHICK-PEAS

SERVES 4

Chick-peas are a great source of carbohydrate and are important in a vegetarian diet. Here they are simmered in a spicy tomato sauce and are delicious served with brown rice.

200 g (7 oz) chick-peas

5 g (1 tsp) bicarbonate of soda

1 onion, halved and sliced

2.5 cm (1 in) piece of root ginger, grated

4 tomatoes, chopped

1 green chilli, chopped

5 g (1 tsp) curry powder

2.5 g (½ tsp) chilli powder

5 g (1 tsp) ground coriander

300 ml (½ pint) vegetable stock

fresh chopped coriander to garnish

NUTRITION FACTS	
Serving Size 1 (274g)	
Calories 250	K Calories from Fat 36
	% Daily Value
Total Fat 4g	6%
Saturated Fat 1g	5%
Monounsaturated Fat 1.4g	0%
Polyunsaturated Fat 0.9g	0%
Cholesterol 4mg	1%
Sodium 709mg	30%
Total Carbohydrate 42g	14%
Dietary Fibre 4g	15%
Sugars 7g	0%
Protein 14g	0%

Per cent daily values are based on a 2000 calorie diet

≈ Put the chick-peas in a large mixing bowl with the bicarbonate of soda and enough water to cover. Leave to soak overnight. Drain the chick-peas and cover with fresh water in a large saucepan. Bring to the boil and boil rapidly for 10 minutes. Reduce the heat and simmer for 1 hour or until cooked.

≈ Drain the chick-peas and put in a non-stick frying pan with the remaining ingredients. Cover and simmer for 20 minutes, stirring occasionally. Garnish with coriander and serve with brown rice.

WINTER VEGETABLE CASSEROLE

SERVES 4

This recipe makes use of many winter vegetables, but use whatever you have to hand as long as there is a good mixture. Cauliflower helps to thicken the sauce slightly, therefore it is always best to include this in your recipe.

2 large potatoes, sliced

900 ml (1½ pints) vegetable stock

2 carrots, cut into chunks

1 onion, sliced

2 garlic cloves, crushed

2 parsnips, cored and sliced

1 leek, sliced

2 celery sticks, sliced

175 g (6 oz) cauliflower florets

salt and ground black pepper

5 g (1 tsp) paprika

30 g (2 tbsp) fresh chopped mixed
    herbs

25 g (1 oz) low-fat vegetarian
    cheese, grated

≈ Cook the potatoes in boiling water for 10 minutes. Drain well and reserve. Meanwhile, heat 300 ml (½ pint) of the stock in a flameproof casserole dish. Add all of the vegetables, remaining stock, seasoning, and paprika and cook for 15 minutes stirring occasionally. Add the herbs and adjust the seasoning.

≈ Lay the potato slices on top of the vegetable mixture and sprinkle the cheese on top. Cook in the oven at 190°C (375°F, Gas 5) for 30 minutes or until the top is golden brown and the cheese has melted. Serve with a salad.

NUTRITION FACTS	
Serving Size 1 (479g)	
Calories 180	Calories from Fat 27
	% Daily Value
Total Fat 3g	5%
Saturated Fat 0g	1%
Monounsaturated Fat 0.8g	0%
Polyunsaturated Fat 0.5g	0%
Cholesterol 0mg	0%
Sodium 1520mg	63%
Total Carbohydrate 35g	12%
Dietary Fibre 5g	22%
Sugars 9g	0%
Protein 8g	0%

Per cent daily values are based on a 2000 calorie diet

ROAST PEPPER TART

SERVES 8

This is one of those dishes that is as appealing to the eye as to the palate. A medley of roast peppers in a cheese sauce are served in a crisp filo pastry case. For a dinner party, make individual pastry cases and serve the tarts with a small salad.

225 g (8 oz) filo pastry
225 g (8 oz) margarine, melted

For the filling
2 red peppers, seeded and halved
2 green peppers, seeded and halved
2 garlic cloves, crushed

For the sauce
300 ml (½ pint) skimmed milk
25 g (1 oz) low-fat vegetarian
    cheese, grated
30 g (2 tbsp) cornflour
50 ml (4 fl oz) vegetable stock
15 g (1 tbsp) fresh snipped chives
15 g (1 tbsp) fresh chopped basil
1 garlic clove, crushed
5 ml (1 tsp) wholegrain mustard
basil and chives to garnish

NUTRITION FACTS	
Serving Size 1 (150g)	
Calories 150	Calories from Fat 36
	% Daily Value
Total Fat 4g	6%
Saturated Fat 1g	3%
Monounsaturated Fat 1.4g	0%
Polyunsaturated Fat 1.5g	0%
Cholesterol 1mg	0%
Sodium 235mg	10%
Total Carbohydrate 23g	8%
Dietary Fibre 1g	2%
Sugars 2g	0%
Protein 5g	0%

Per cent daily values are based on a 2000 calorie diet

≈ Lay two sheets of filo pastry in a pie plate allowing the pastry to overhang the sides a little. Brush with margarine and lay another two sheets on top at opposite angles. Brush with margarine and continue in this way until all of the pastry has been used. Heat the oven to 200°C (400°F, Gas 6) and cook the pastry case for 15 minutes until golden and crisp.

≈ Meanwhile, lay the peppers on a baking sheet, skin side uppermost. Sprinkle the garlic over the peppers, cook in the oven for 20 minutes. Allow to cool slightly then peel the peppers, discarding the skin. Cut the peppers into strips and place in the pastry case.

≈ Heat the milk for the sauce in a pan, add the cheese and stir until melted. Blend the cornflour with 4 tablespoons cold water and stir into the sauce to form a paste. Bring to the boil, stirring until thickened and add the remaining ingredients with the stock. Spoon the sauce over the peppers, garnish with basil and chives and serve.

PASTA TIMBALE

SERVES 8

This is a really different way to serve pasta in a courgette-lined mould which is baked until set and served with a tomato sauce.

≈ Cut the courgettes into thin strips with a vegetable peeler and blanch in boiling water for 2–3 minutes. Refresh the courgettes under cold water, then put in a bowl and cover with cold water until required.

≈ Cook the pasta in boiling salted water for 8–10 minutes until just tender. Drain well and reserve.

≈ Heat the stock in a saucepan and cook the onions, garlic, carrot, corn and pepper for 5 minutes. Stir in the pasta, cheese, tomatoes, eggs and oregano, season well and cook for 3 minutes, stirring well.

≈ Line a 1.2 litre (2 pint) mould or round tin with the courgette strips, covering the base and sides and allowing the strips to overhang the sides. Spoon the pasta mixture into the mould and fold the courgette strips over the pasta to cover.

≈ Stand the mould in a roasting tin half filled with boiling water, cover, and cook in the oven at 180°C (350°F, Gas 4) for 30–40 minutes until set.

≈ Meanwhile, put all of the sauce ingredients in a pan and bring to the boil, reduce the heat and cook for 10 minutes. Sieve the sauce into a clean pan and heat gently.

≈ Remove the pasta dish from the oven and carefully turn out of the mould on to a serving plate. Serve with the tomato sauce.

2 courgettes

115 g (4 oz) pasta shapes such as macaroni or penne

90 ml (6 tbsp) vegetable stock

2 onions, chopped

2 garlic cloves, crushed

1 carrot, chopped

30 g (2 tbsp) drained, canned corn

1 green pepper, seeded and chopped

25 g (1 oz) low-fat vegetarian cheese, grated

450 g (16 oz) can chopped tomatoes

2 eggs, beaten

30 g (2 tbsp) fresh chopped oregano

For the sauce

1 onion, chopped

450 g (1 lb) tomatoes, chopped

10 g (2 tsp) granulated sugar

30 ml (2 tbsp) tomato purée

175 ml (6 fl oz) vegetable stock

NUTRITION FACTS	
Serving Size 1 (219g)	
Calories 100	Calories from Fat 27
	% Daily Value
Total Fat 3g	5%
Saturated Fat 1g	3%
Monounsaturated Fat 0.9g	0%
Polyunsaturated Fat 0.4g	0%
Cholesterol 58mg	19%
Sodium 451mg	19%
Total Carbohydrate 14g	5%
Dietary Fibre 2g	9%
Sugars 3g	0%
Protein 6g	0%

Per cent daily values are based on a 2000 calorie diet

VEGETABLE RISOTTO

SERVES 4

Risotto is an Italian dish of cooked rice and either vegetables or meat. It has a creamy texture which is due to the special arborio risotto rice used. The recipe really does call for this but if you do not have any to hand it will still taste great with brown rice.

25 g (1½ tbsp) polyunsaturated margarine

1 onion, halved and sliced

225 g (8 oz) firm, lite tofu, cubed

225 g (8 oz) arborio rice

2.5 ml (½ tsp) turmeric

5 ml (1 tsp) soya sauce

600 ml (1 pint) vegetable stock

1 green chilli, sliced

1 red pepper, seeded, halved and sliced

50 g (2 oz) mangetout

75 g (3 oz) canned waterchestnuts, drained and halved

40 g (1½ oz) oyster mushrooms

NUTRITION FACTS	
Serving Size 1 (372g)	
Calories 182	Calories from Fat 54
	% Daily Value
Total Fat 6g	9%
Saturated Fat 1g	5%
Monounsaturated Fat 2.1g	0%
Polyunsaturated Fat 1.8g	0%
Cholesterol 0mg	0%
Sodium 911mg	38%
Total Carbohydrate 26g	9%
Dietary Fibre 1g	5%
Sugars 2g	0%
Protein 8g	0%

Per cent daily values are based on a 2000 calorie diet

≈ Heat the margarine in a non-stick frying pan and cook the onion and tofu for 3 minutes. Add the rice and turmeric and cook for a further 2 minutes.

≈ Add the soya sauce to the pan with the stock, chilli, pepper, mangetout and waterchestnuts. Bring the mixture to the boil, reduce the heat to a simmer and cook for 15–20 minutes until all of the vegetables are tender. Top the pan up with hot water or stock if required and stir frequently. Stir in the mushrooms and cook for 5 minutes and serve.

VEGETABLE CHOP SUEY

SERVES 4

Add a touch of China to your table with this simple recipe. Vegetables are cooked in a spiced soya sauce and served with brown rice for a quick and healthy meal.

≈ Pour the vegetable stock into a large frying pan or wok with the Chinese five spice powder and cook all of the vegetables except the mushrooms and beansprouts for 5 minutes.

≈ Add the mushrooms, bean sprouts and soya sauce to the pan and cook for a further 5 minutes, stirring well. Serve immediately with boiled brown rice.

300 ml (½ pint) vegetable stock

5 g (1 tsp) Chinese five spice powder

3 carrots, cut into strips

3 celery sticks, sliced

1 red onion, sliced

1 green pepper, seeded and cut into chunks

40 g (1½ oz) open cap mushrooms, sliced

225 g (8 oz) bean sprouts

15 ml (1 tbsp) light soya sauce

NUTRITION FACTS	
Serving Size 1 (250g)	
Calories 57	Calories from Fat 9
	% Daily Value
Total Fat 1g	1%
Saturated Fat 0g	0%
Monounsaturated Fat 0.1g	0%
Polyunsaturated Fat 0.3g	0%
Cholesterol 0mg	0%
Sodium 620mg	26%
Total Carbohydrate 10g	3%
Dietary Fibre 3g	10%
Sugars 4g	0%
Protein 4g	0%

Per cent daily values are based on a 2000 calorie diet

TOFU BURGERS AND CHIPS

SERVES 4

Here is a recipe that low-fat dieters dream of. Although not chips in the strictest sense, these blanched potato sticks are tossed in flour and a little oil and baked to crispness in the oven.

≈ Boil the carrots in water for 10–12 minutes until soft. Drain really well. Cook the cabbage in boiling water for 5 minutes and drain really well. Put the carrots, cabbage, onion, tofu and coriander in a food processor and blend for 10 seconds. Using floured hands form the mixture into four equal-sized burgers. Chill in the refrigerator for 1 hour or until firm.

≈ Cut the potatoes into thick chips and cook in boiling water for 10 minutes. Drain well and toss in the flour. Put the potatoes in a plastic bag and sprinkle in the oil. Seal the top of the bag and shake the fries to coat. Turn the potatoes out on to a non-stick baking sheet. Cook in the oven at 200°C (400°F, Gas 6) for 30 minutes or until golden brown.

≈ Meanwhile, place the burgers under a hot grill for 7–8 minutes, turning with a fish slice. Toast the burger buns for 2 minutes and place a burger on one half. Add the tomatoes, lettuce and onion and serve with the chips.

For the burgers

185 g (6½ oz) carrots, chopped

50 g (2 oz) cabbage, shredded

1 onion, chopped

275 g (10 oz) firm, lite tofu, cubed

5 g (1 tsp) ground coriander

4 burger buns split

sliced tomatoes, lettuce and onion

For the fries

2 large potatoes

30 g (2 tbsp) flour

15 ml (1 tbsp) sunflower oil

NUTRITION FACTS	
Serving Size 1 (459g)	
Calories 280	Calories from Fat 63
	% Daily Value
Total Fat 7g	11%
Saturated Fat 1g	5%
Monounsaturated Fat 2.0g	0%
Polyunsaturated Fat 3.0g	0%
Cholesterol 0mg	0%
Sodium 218mg	9%
Total Carbohydrate 38g	13%
Dietary Fibre 5g	20%
Sugars 8g	0%
Protein 17g	0%

Per cent daily values are based on a 2000 calorie diet

CAULIFLOWER BAKED WITH TOMATOES AND FETA CHEESE

SERVES 4

This dish is enlivened with a strong flavour of tomatoes combined with the typically Greek use of ground cinnamon.

6 tbsp olive oil

1 onion, sliced

2 garlic cloves, crushed

8 tomatoes, peeled and chopped

large pinch of ground cinnamon

2 tsp dried oregano

salt and freshly ground black pepper, to taste

1 large cauliflower, cut into florets

1 tbsp freshly squeezed lemon juice

80 g/3 oz feta cheese, grated

≈ Heat 2–3 tbsp olive oil in a heavy-based pan and sauté the onion and garlic for 3–4 minutes, or until the onion has softened.

≈ Add the chopped tomatoes, cinnamon and oregano and season with salt and pepper. Stir and simmer, covered, for 5 minutes.

≈ Preheat the oven to 190°C/375°F/ Gas Mark 5. Add the cauliflower to the tomato mixture, cover, and simmer for a further 10–15 minutes or until the cauliflower is just tender. Remove from the heat.

≈ Transfer the cauliflower and tomato mixture to a large, shallow dish and drizzle over the remaining olive oil. Sprinkle over the lemon juice and grated feta. Bake for 45–50 minutes, or until the cauliflower is soft and the cheese has melted. Serve warm.

NUTRITION FACTS	
Amount per Serving	
Calories 250	Calories from Fat 190
	% Daily Value
Total Fat 21g	32%
Saturated Fat 5g	25%
Polyunsaturated Fat 2g	0%
Monounsaturated Fat 13g	0%
Cholesterol 13mg	4%
Sodium 290mg	12%
Total Carbohydrate 9g	3%
Dietary Fibre 4g	16%
Sugars 8g	0%
Protein 6.5g	0%

Percent daily values are based on a 2000 calorie diet

104

GREEN LENTILS WITH CARROT, ONION AND GARLIC

SERVES 6

Green lentils are recommended for this dish because the green variety will only disintegrate after extreme provocation. If you are using red lentils, cook them carefully and remove them from the heat while they are still firm and in one piece.

450 g/1 lb green lentils

4 tbsp olive oil

1 large onion

2 cloves garlic

1 medium carrot

3 tbsp flour

1 pinch each thyme, parsley, sage

salt and pepper to taste

≈ Wash the lentils thoroughly in cold water and then boil them until soft. Reserve the lentils, in their pan, until needed.

≈ While the lentils are cooking, chop the onion, crush the garlic, and slice the carrot into thin strips.

≈ In another saucepan, heat the oil over a medium heat and add the onion, the garlic and the carrot. Cook the vegetables until the onions begin to brown, then stir in the flour and cook until golden.

≈ Now lift the lentils from their cooking juices and stir them into the saucepan with the vegetables. Gradually add small amounts of the lentil stock until you have a stew the consistency of thin cream.

≈ Season to taste with the herbs, salt and pepper and serve.

NUTRITION FACTS	
Amount per Serving	
Calories 335	Calories from Fat 80
	% Daily Value
Total Fat 9g	14%
Saturated Fat 1g	5%
Polyunsaturated Fat 1g	0%
Monounsaturated Fat 6g	0%
Cholesterol 0mg	0%
Sodium 14mg	0.6%
Total Carbohydrate 47g	16%
Dietary Fibre 11g	44%
Sugars 3g	0%
Protein 20g	0%

Percent daily values are based on a 2000 calorie diet

PEPPERS WITH GNOCCHI

SERVES 4

A refreshing alternative to rice, pasta makes a perfect filling for peppers. Tiny pasta shapes also work well in this dish. Serve with a crisp green salad.

225 g/½ lb small gnocchi (small dumpling shapes)
dash of olive oil
4 peppers, for stuffing
parsley sprigs, to garnish

Filling

50 ml/2 fl oz olive oil
6 spring onions, finely chopped
2 cloves of garlic, crushed
1 pepper, seeded and finely diced
salt and freshly ground black pepper
80 g/3 oz freshly grated Parmesan cheese

≈ Bring a large pan of water to the boil, and add the pasta with a dash of olive oil. Cook for 10 minutes, until tender. Drain.

≈ Preheat the oven to 200°C/400°F/ Gas Mark 6. Lay each pepper on its side and slice off the top, reserving it to make the lid. Scoop out and discard the seeds and pith. Arrange the hollowed-out peppers in a shallow, ovenproof dish, and set aside.

≈ To make the filling, heat the oil and sauté the spring onions and garlic for 2 minutes, then add the diced pepper. Season with salt and pepper and cook for 5 minutes, stirring occasionally.

≈ Add the gnocchi and the Parmesan cheese to the filling mixture, and cook for about 2 minutes to heat through. Using a tablespoon, stuff each pepper with the pasta filling, scattering any extra around the edges.

≈ Place the pepper lids on each pepper and bake for about 30 minutes, until the peppers have softened. Just before serving, place under the grill for 2–3 minutes to char the pepper skins, if desired. Serve garnished with parsley sprigs.

NUTRITION FACTS	
Amount per Serving	
Calories 436	Calories from Fat 170
	% Daily Value
Total Fat 19g	29%
Saturated Fat 8g	40%
Polyunsaturated Fat 2g	0%
Monounsaturated Fat 8g	0%
Cholesterol 31mg	10%
Sodium 357mg	15%
Total Carbohydrate 49g	16%
Dietary Fibre 8g	32%
Sugars 7g	0%
Protein 21g	0%

Percent daily values are based on a 2000 calorie diet

SPICY OKRA AND MANGO

SERVES 4

Serve this with fairly substantial fresh pasta shapes – fresh rigatoni for example – or the dried types, which tend to be a bit thicker when cooked.

225 g/8 oz small, young okra

4 tsp ground coriander

1 large firm mango

3 tbsp olive oil

1 large onion, chopped

1 large red pepper, seeded, halved lengthwise and sliced

2 garlic cloves, crushed

2 green chilli peppers, seeded and chopped

4 tsp chopped fresh oregano

salt and freshly ground black pepper

1 lime, cut into wedges, to serve

≈ The okra must be small, firm, bright in colour and unblemished. Old fibrous or large okra will not cook successfully. Trim the stalk ends and points off the pods, then slice them thinly, and put in a bowl. Add the coriander, and toss well.

≈ The mango should be just ripe, but still firm (fruit that is soft or too sweet will not complement the okra). Peel the mango; then slice the flesh off the large, flat central pit. Cut the slices into small pieces.

≈ Heat the oil in a saucepan. Add the onion, pepper, garlic, chilli peppers and oregano; then cook, stirring occasionally for 10 minutes. Stir in the okra, and cook over a fairly high heat for about 3–5 minutes, until the okra slices are slightly browned in part, and just tender. Stir in the mango, taste for seasoning, and serve. Toss the okra mixture with the pasta; then arrange lime wedges around the edge of the dish so that their juice may be squeezed over to taste.

NUTRITION FACTS	
Amount per Serving	
Calories 135	Calories from Fat 80
	% Daily Value
Total Fat 9g	14%
Saturated Fat 1g	5%
Polyunsaturated Fat 1g	0%
Monounsaturated Fat 6g	0%
Cholesterol 0mg	0%
Sodium 17mg	0.7%
Total Carbohydrate 11g	4%
Dietary Fibre 1.5g	6%
Sugars 8g	0%
Protein 3g	0%

Percent daily values are based on a 2000 calorie diet

PASTA-STUFFED CABBAGE LEAVES

SERVES 4

Easy to prepare and sure to impress guests, this dish can be made a day in advance and kept in the refrigerator. Allow an extra 15–20 minutes to reheat in the oven before serving.

50 g/2 oz dried gnocchetti sardi (dumpling shapes) and/or pastina (any tiny shapes)

dash of olive oil

8 large savoy cabbage leaves, stalks removed

Filling

2 tbsp olive oil

2 cloves of garlic, crushed

2 carrots, peeled and grated

2 courgettes, grated

4 tomatoes, skinned, seeded, and chopped

50 g/2 oz chopped walnuts

salt and freshly ground black pepper

Sauce

400 g/14-oz can chopped tomatoes

4 tbsp dry red wine

150 ml/5 fl oz vegetable stock

1 tbsp dried oregano

1 onion, very finely chopped

salt and freshly ground black pepper

≈ Bring a large saucepan of water to the boil, and add the pasta with a dash of olive oil. Cook for about 10 minutes, stirring occasionally, until tender. Drain and set aside.

≈ Blanch the cabbage leaves in boiling water, then quickly immerse in cold water and drain. Pat dry with paper towels, and set aside.

≈ To make the filling, heat the olive oil in a large frying pan and sauté the garlic for about 1 minute. Add the grated carrots and courgettes, and cook for a further 3–4 minutes, stirring occasionally, until tender.

≈ Add the chopped tomatoes, walnuts and pasta. Season with salt and freshly ground black pepper. Cook for about 5 minutes, stirring occasionally, then set aside to cool.

≈ To make the sauce, place all the ingredients in a saucepan and bring to a simmer. Cook for 20–30 minutes, stirring occasionally, until reduced and thickened. Allow to cool slightly, then transfer to a food processor or blender and purée until smooth. Set aside.

≈ Preheat the oven to 200°C/400°F/Gas Mark 6.

≈ To assemble the stuffed cabbage leaves, lay the blanched leaves out on a work surface, concave side uppermost, and divide the mixture among the leaves, placing some of it in the centre of each leaf. Fold the edges of each leaf over to completely encase the filling.

≈ Arrange the stuffed leaves in a shallow ovenproof dish, and pour the sauce around the edges. Cover with foil and bake for about 20 minutes, until heated through. Serve immediately, with any extra sauce served separately.

NUTRITION FACTS	
Amount per Serving	
Calories 266	Calories from Fat 145
	% Daily Value
Total Fat 16g	25%
Saturated Fat 2g	10%
Polyunsaturated Fat 6.5g	0%
Monounsaturated Fat 6g	0%
Cholesterol 0mg	0%
Sodium 64mg	3%
Total Carbohydrate 23g	8%
Dietary Fibre 8g	32%
Sugars 13g	0%
Protein 7g	0%

Percent daily values are based on a 2000 calorie diet

AUBERGINE RAGOUT

SERVES 4

This richly flavoured dish should be accompanied at the table by plenty of fresh bread, feta cheese and a full-bodied red wine.

3 aubergines

salt

125 ml/4 fl oz olive oil

2 onions, halved and sliced

4 garlic cloves, crushed

675 g/1½ lb tomatoes, peeled, seeded, and chopped

3 tbsp chopped fresh parsley

salt and freshly ground black pepper, to taste

NUTRITION FACTS	
Amount per Serving	
Calories 302	Calories from Fat 250
	% Daily Value
Total Fat 28g	43%
Saturated Fat 4g	20%
Polyunsaturated Fat 3g	0%
Monounsaturated Fat 20g	0%
Cholesterol 0mg	0%
Sodium 18mg	0.75%
Total Carbohydrate 10g	3%
Dietary Fibre 6g	24%
Sugars 9g	0%
Protein 3g	0%

Percent daily values are based on a 2000 calorie diet

≈ Cut the aubergine into thick chunks and place in a colander. Generously sprinkle with salt and set aside for 30–45 minutes. Rinse the aubergine under cold running water and drain well.

≈ Heat the olive oil in a large saucepan and add the onion. Cook for 3–5 minutes, or until the onion has softened, then add the aubergine; stir to coat.

≈ Add the garlic, tomatoes and parsley to the saucepan and season with salt and freshly ground black pepper. Add a little water to moisten the mixture, if necessary, then cover and simmer for about 50–55 minutes, or until the aubergine is very soft and the sauce has thickened. Serve warm or cold.

BAKED MIXED VEGETABLES

SERVES 6

This light and easy-to-prepare dish is a favourite throughout Greece during spring and summer.

6 tbsp olive oil

3 onions, sliced

675 g/1½ lb small potatoes, peeled and halved, or cut into thick slices

675 g/1½ lb courgettes, cut into chunks

8 ripe tomatoes, peeled and roughly chopped

2 peppers, seeded and sliced into rings

4 garlic cloves, finely chopped

1 tsp dried oregano

4 tbsp chopped fresh parsley

2 tbsp chopped fresh dill

salt and freshly ground black pepper, to taste

125 ml/4 fl oz water

≈ Preheat the oven to 180°C/350°F/ Gas Mark 4. Heat 2 tbsp of the olive oil in a skillet and sauté the onion for 3–5 minutes, until softened but not coloured. Remove from the heat.

≈ Combine the sautéed onion with the prepared potatoes, courgettes, tomatoes, peppers, garlic, herbs and seasoning in a large roasting pan. Add the water and bake for 1½–2 hours, until the vegetables are tender and cooked through. Stir the vegetables around occasionally to cook through evenly. Serve warm or cold.

NUTRITION FACTS	
Amount per Serving	
Calories 239	Calories from Fat 108
	% Daily Value
Total Fat 12g	18%
Saturated Fat 2g	10%
Polyunsaturated Fat 2g	0%
Monounsaturated Fat 8g	0%
Cholesterol 0mg	0%
Sodium 27mg	1%
Total Carbohydrate 28g	9%
Dietary Fibre 7g	28%
Sugars 10g	0%
Protein 6g	0%

Percent daily values are based on a 2000 calorie diet

LAYERED AUBERGINE, POTATO AND TOMATO CASSEROLE

SERVES 6

In the Mediterranean aubergine dishes date from the time of the Moors. This one must have been updated when tomatoes, peppers and potatoes were introduced from America. It is typical of the solid soups and vegetable dishes of the islands, made in the earthenware greixonera.

2 aubergines

salt and freshly ground black pepper

9 small potatoes, peeled and sliced

2 large onions, chopped

100 ml/4 fl oz olive oil

2 garlic cloves, finely chopped

2 green peppers, seeded and sliced

1 red pepper, seeded and sliced

4 tbsp chopped parsley

3 400 g/14-oz cans tomatoes

2 tsp paprika

60 ml/2 fl oz red-wine vinegar

≈ Slice the aubergines very thinly, lay the slices out on a cutting board, and sprinkle with salt. Leave to sweat for 30–40 minutes, then blot with paper towels. Prepare the potatoes and cook them for 15 minutes in boiling salted water. Soften the onions in 2 tbsp oil over a low heat, then add the garlic.

≈ Grease an earthenware dish or casserole (30 cm/12 in across, by 7 cm/ 3 in deep) with oil. Make three layers of vegetables, starting with a third of the potato slices, then the aubergine slices, then the peppers, cooked onion and garlic, plus parsley. Add 1 can tomatoes and juice, squeezing the tomatoes through clenched fingers to break them up well. Season with salt, pepper and the paprika. Repeat until all ingredients are in. Sprinkle vinegar over the second layer and 1–1½ tbsps of oil over the top of the dish.

≈ Cover with foil and bake in a preheated oven at 200°C/400°F/ Gas Mark 6 for 1 hour. Then remove the foil, turn down the heat to 170°C/325°F/Gas Mark 3, and give it another 30–60 minutes, to brown and concentrate the juices. Excellent hot or cold, this dish also reheats well.

NUTRITION FACTS

Amount per Serving

Calories 267	Calories from Fat 170
	% Daily Value
Total Fat 19g	29%
Saturated Fat 3g	15%
Polyunsaturated Fat 2g	0%
Monounsaturated Fat 13g	0%
Cholesterol 0mg	0%
Sodium 90mg	3%
Total Carbohydrate 20.5g	7%
Dietary Fibre 6.5g	26%
Sugars 12g	0%
Protein 4.5g	0%

Percent daily values are based on a 2000 calorie diet

PROVENÇAL GREEN BEANS WITH PASTA

SERVES 4

A delicious way to serve green beans, piping hot with freshly grated Parmesan cheese.

3 tbsp olive oil

3 cloves of garlic, crushed

1 onion, chopped

3 tbsp chopped, fresh thyme

450 g/1 lb green beans

400 g/14-oz can chopped tomatoes

2 heaped tbsp tomato paste

450 ml/16 fl oz vegetable stock

150 ml/5 fl oz dry red wine

salt and freshly ground black pepper

450 g/1 lb dried pasta (any shapes)

freshly grated Parmesan cheese

≈ Heat 2 tbsp oil in a large pan and sauté the garlic and onion for about 3 minutes until softened. Add the thyme, beans, tomatoes, tomato paste, vegetable stock and wine, season with salt and freshly ground black pepper, and stir well to combine.

≈ Cover and cook gently for 25–30 minutes, until the beans are tender. Remove the lid and cook for a further 5–8 minutes, stirring occasionally, until the sauce has thickened slightly.

≈ Meanwhile, bring a large saucepan of water to the boil, and add the pasta with a dash of olive oil. Cook for about 10 minutes, stirring occasionally, until tender. Drain and return to the saucepan. Toss in oil and freshly ground black pepper.

≈ Serve the beans with the hot, buttered pasta and freshly grated Parmesan cheese.

NUTRITION FACTS	
Amount per Serving	
Calories 598	Calories from Fat 135
	% Daily Value
Total Fat 15g	23%
Saturated Fat 3g	15%
Polyunsaturated Fat 2g	0%
Monounsaturated Fat 9g	0%
Cholesterol 5mg	2%
Sodium 133mg	5.5%
Total Carbohydrate 95g	32%
Dietary Fibre 10g	40%
Sugars 10g	0%
Protein 20g	0%

Percent daily values are based on a 2000 calorie diet

FUSILLI WITH SUN-DRIED TOMATOES

SERVES 4

A dish that is delicious served warm as a main course or cold as a summer salad.

450 g/1 lb dried fusilli (pasta twists)

olive oil

2 tbsp tomato pesto

175 g/6-oz jar sun-dried tomatoes,
    drained and chopped

4 plum tomatoes, sliced into wedges

4 tbsp chopped, fresh basil

salt and freshly ground black pepper

≈ Bring a large saucepan of water to the boil and add the pasta with a dash of olive oil. Cook for about 10 minutes, stirring occasionally until tender. Drain and return to the saucepan.

≈ Stir in the remaining ingredients, drizzle with olive oil and serve warm immediately, or cool and refrigerate to serve chilled, if preferred.

NUTRITION FACTS	
Amount per Serving	
Calories 673	Calories from Fat 270
	% Daily Value
Total Fat 30g	46%
Saturated Fat 4.5g	22%
Polyunsaturated Fat 14g	0%
Monounsaturated Fat 9g	0%
Cholesterol 3mg	1%
Sodium 494mg	20%
Total Carbohydrate 90g	30%
Dietary Fibre 6g	24%
Sugars 6g	0%
Protein 17g	0%

Percent daily values are based on a 2000 calorie diet

KIDNEY BEAN, ARTICHOKE AND MUSHROOM CASSEROLE

SERVES 4

175 g/6 oz kidney beans

1–2 tbsp oil

1 large onion, chopped

1–2 cloves garlic, chopped

225 g/8 oz mushrooms, sliced

175 g/6 oz green beans, trimmed,
    cut in thirds and parboiled

425 g/15-oz can artichoke hearts

425 g/15-oz can tomatoes, mashed

salt and freshly ground black pepper

parsley

≈ Soak the kidney beans overnight and cook until tender.

≈ Preheat the oven to 180°C/350°F/ Gas Mark 4. Heat oil in a pan and fry onion and garlic until translucent. Add the mushrooms and stir-fry for 1–2 minutes until they begin to soften.

≈ Transfer all the ingredients to a casserole. Season well. Cover and bake for 30–40 minutes. Sprinkle with parsley and serve with baked potatoes and a green salad.

NUTRITION FACTS	
Amount per Serving	
Calories 279	Calories from Fat 45
	% Daily Value
Total Fat 5g	8%
Saturated Fat 1g	5%
Polyunsaturated Fat 3g	0%
Monounsaturated Fat 1g	0%
Cholesterol 0mg	0%
Sodium 56mg	2%
Total Carbohydrate 44g	15%
Dietary Fibre 21g	84%
Sugars 8g	0%
Protein 18g	0%

Percent daily values are based on a 2000 calorie diet

SPAGHETTI WITH TOMATOES

SERVES 4

This is a vegetarian version of a simple yet classic Italian dish.

350 g/¾ lb spaghetti (long tubes)

dash of olive oil

2 cloves of garlic, crushed

1 onion, finely chopped

450 g/1 lb carton sieved tomatoes

4 tbsp chopped, fresh basil

salt and freshly ground black pepper

80 g/3 oz freshly grated Parmesan
   cheese

NUTRITION FACTS

Amount per Serving

Calories 511	Calories from Fat 140
	% Daily Value
Total Fat 15.5g	24%
Saturated Fat 8g	40%
Polyunsaturated Fat 1g	0%
Monounsaturated Fat 5g	0%
Cholesterol 38mg	13%
Sodium 430mg	18%
Total Carbohydrate 71g	24%
Dietary Fibre 6g	24%
Sugars 6g	0%
Protein 26g	0%

Percent daily values are based on a 2000 calorie diet

≈ Bring a large saucepan of water to the boil and add the pasta with a dash of olive oil. Cook for about 10 minutes, stirring occasionally until tender. Drain and set aside.

≈ Preheat the oven to 200°C/400°F/ Gas Mark 6. Place the garlic, onion, sieved tomatoes, basil and salt and freshly ground black pepper in a large pan, and heat until simmering. Cook for about 5 minutes, then remove from the heat.

≈ Arrange the pasta in a shallow, oiled, ovenproof dish. Curl it around to fit the dish, until the dish is tightly packed with the pasta.

≈ Spoon the tomato mixture over the top, pushing the pasta to ensure the sauce sinks down to the bottom of the dish. Sprinkle with the grated cheese, and bake for 25–30 minutes, until bubbling, crisp and golden. Cut in wedges, like a cake, to serve.

TAGLIATELLE NEAPOLITAN

SERVES 4

Yellow tomatoes make this dish look particularly attractive, although red ones taste just as good. If you can't find fresh tagliatelle, use the dried egg version.

450 g/1 lb fresh, multicoloured
    tagliatelle
dash of olive oil, plus 2 tbsp
2 cloves of garlic, crushed
1 onion, chopped
3 tbsp chopped, fresh basil or
    oregano
450 g/1 lb yellow and red tomatoes,
    skinned, seeded and chopped
225 g/8-oz carton chopped tomatoes
salt and freshly ground black pepper
fresh basil, to garnish
freshly grated Parmesan cheese, to
    serve

≈ Bring a large saucepan of water to the boil and add the tagliatelle with a dash of olive oil. Cook for about 5 minutes, stirring occasionally until tender. Drain and set aside, covered.

≈ Heat the remaining oil in a large pan, and sauté the garlic, onion and basil or oregano for about 3 minutes, or until the onion has softened.

≈ Add the chopped tomato flesh and drained tomatoes and season with salt and freshly ground black pepper. Stir and cook for about 10 minutes, until thickened and bubbling. Serve with the tagliatelle. Garnish with fresh basil and sprinkle with freshly grated Parmesan cheese.

NUTRITION FACTS	
Amount per Serving	
Calories 510	Calories from Fat 100

	% Daily Value
Total Fat 11g	17%
Saturated Fat 2g	10%
Polyunsaturated Fat 2g	0%
Monounsaturated Fat 6g	0%
Cholesterol 5mg	2%
Sodium 100mg	4%
Total Carbohydrate 92g	31%
Dietary Fibre 7g	28%
Sugars 8g	0%
Protein 17g	0%

Percent daily values are based on a 2000 calorie diet

POTATOES WITH CHICKPEAS

SERVES 6

This is another popular, filling dish, which can do service as a side dish if served without the fresh spinach that is stirred into the potatoes and chickpeas in the last 5 minutes of cooking.

4 oz (100 ml) olive oil

1 large onion, chopped

12 oz (340 g) small red potatoes,
    washed and cut into small pieces

2 garlic cloves, finely chopped

1 lb (450 g) cooked and drained
    chickpeas

1 lb (450 g) fresh spinach, chopped

5 medium tomatoes, peeled, seeded
    and chopped

cayenne pepper

½ tsp coriander seeds

salt and freshly ground pepper

3 tbsp finely chopped fresh parsley

≈ Heat the olive oil in an ovenproof casserole with a cover. Add the onion and cook until it is lightly coloured and limp.

≈ Add the chopped potatoes and the garlic, and cook, stirring, over low heat for 3–4 minutes. Stir in the chickpeas, the tomatoes, cayenne pepper to taste, and the coriander seeds.

≈ Cover and simmer for 15–20 minutes, or until the potatoes are soft. Stir in the fresh spinach in the last 5 minutes of cooking and leave to wilt. Season to taste and stir in the chopped parsley before serving.

≈ This dish can also be cooled, chilled overnight, and served cold.

NUTRITION FACTS	
Amount per Serving	
Calories 293	Calories from Fat 198
	% Daily Value
Total Fat 22g	34%
Saturated Fat 3g	15%
Polyunsaturated Fat 2.5g	0%
Monounsaturated Fat 15g	0%
Cholesterol 0mg	0%
Sodium 120mg	5%
Total Carbohydrate 20g	7%
Dietary Fibre 4g	16%
Sugars 5g	0%
Protein 6g	0%

Percent daily values are based on a 2000 calorie diet

POTATO-TOPPED VEGETABLE PIE

SERVES 4

Cook the potatoes whole in their skins to retain maximum nutrients; once cooked they can easily be peeled and mashed. This dish can be prepared the previous day if necessary.

3 oz (85 g) green lentils, washed and drained

1 lb (450 g) barley, washed and drained

1 medium onion, chopped

14-oz (300-g) tin chopped tomatoes

12 oz (340 g) cauliflower florets

2 celery stalks, sliced

1 leek, thickly sliced

1 turnip, thinly sliced

2 carrots, diced

2 tsp mixed dry herbs

1½ lb (675 g) potatoes, scrubbed

3 tbsp low-fat milk

salt and freshly ground black pepper

1½ oz (40 g) low-fat medium-hard cheese, grated

≈ Set the oven to 205°C/400°F/Gas 6. Place the lentils, barley, onion, tomatoes (with juice), cauliflower, celery, leek, turnip, carrots and herbs in a large saucepan and add ½ pint (¼ litre) water. Bring to a boil, cover and simmer for 40–45 minutes or until the lentils, barley and vegetables are just tender.

≈ Cook the potatoes in boiling, salted water for about 20 minutes, or until they are soft. Drain, peel, and mash them with the milk, and season to taste.

≈ Place the lentil mixture in a baking dish and pipe or fork the mashed potato on top to cover. Sprinkle the cheese on top, and bake the pie in the oven for 30–35 minutes, until it is evenly light brown. Serve hot. A tomato and herb salad makes a good accompaniment.*

NUTRITION FACTS	
Amount per Serving	
Calories 355	Calories from Fat 27
	% Daily Value
Total Fat 3g	5%
Saturated Fat 1g	5%
Polyunsaturated Fat 1g	0%
Monounsaturated Fat 0.5g	0%
Cholesterol 4mg	1.3%
Sodium 142mg	6%
Total Carbohydrate 70g	23%
Dietary Fibre 10g	40%
Sugars 11g	0%
Protein 16g	0%

Percent daily values are based on a 2000 calorie diet

BAKED MUSHROOM BURGERS

SERVES 4

These vegetable burgers freeze well, and can be cooked without thawing first. If frozen, add 5 minutes to the cooking time.

6 fl oz (175 ml) vegetable stock

2 medium onions, finely chopped

2 cloves garlic, crushed

½ lb (225 g) mushrooms, trimmed
    and finely chopped

2 tbsp fine oatmeal

4 oz (115 g) rolled oats

1 tbsp tomato purée

salt and freshly ground black pepper

2 tbsp chopped walnuts

2 tbsp chopped mint

Coating

a little skimmed milk

about 3 oz (75 g) rolled oats

Garnish

1–2 tbsp chopped mint

tomato wedges (optional)

NUTRITION FACTS	
Amount per Serving	
Calories 177	Calories from Fat 60
	% Daily Value
Total Fat 6.5g	10%
Saturated Fat 0.7g	3.5%
Polyunsaturated Fat 3g	0%
Monounsaturated Fat 1g	0%
Cholesterol 0mg	0%
Sodium 22mg	9%
Total Carbohydrate 25g	8%
Dietary Fibre 5g	20%
Sugars 4g	0%
Protein 6g	0%

Percent daily values are based on a 2000 calorie diet

≈ Set the oven to 180°C/350°F/Gas 4. Put 6 tablespoons of the stock in a pan, add the onion and garlic, and bring to a boil. Simmer uncovered for 3–4 minutes, stirring once or twice. Stir in the mushrooms and cook for 3–4 minutes, then add the oatmeal and cook for 1 minute.

≈ Stir in the rolled oats and tomato purée and gradually pour on the remaining stock, stirring constantly. Season with salt and pepper, stir in the walnuts and mint, and remove from the heat. Add a little more stock or skimmed milk if the mixture is too thick; cook it over low heat for a minute or so if it is too runny. It should be a thick paste.

≈ Separate the mixture into 8 pieces, and shape each portion into rounds. Dip each one first in milk and then in rolled oats to cover them evenly on all sides.

≈ Place the burgers on a non-stick baking tray and bake them in the oven for 20–25 minutes, turning them once, until they are well browned. Garnish and serve while still hot.

MUSHROOM AND BROCCOLI NUT LOAF

SERVES 4

With its colourful layer of broccoli spears, this vegetarian loaf is both attractive and appetizing. It is equally good served hot or cold, and freezes well.

≈ Set the oven to 180°C/350°F/Gas 4. Sauté the mushrooms in a pan with half of the margarine. Drain the slices, and place them in a line down the centre of a lightly greased 5 x 7½ x 3 in (12 x 18 x 6 cm) loaf tin.

≈ Cook the celery, garlic and onion in the same pan until softened. Stir in the flour and tomatoes (with juice), and cook until the mixture thickens. Add the breadcrumbs, nuts, egg, herbs and seasoning, and remove from the heat. Spread half of the mixture in the loaf tin. Add the broccoli spears, and top with the remaining mixture.

≈ Cover the tin with foil, place it in a roasting pan half-filled with boiling water, and bake in the oven for 1¼–1½ hours.

≈ For the sauce, melt the remaining margarine, add the chopped mushrooms, and cook for 2–3 minutes. Stir in the flour, and cook for 1 minute. Add the stock, milk and seasoning and stir for 1–2 minutes, until thickened.

≈ Turn out the loaf on to a heated serving dish, and serve the sauce separately. Garnish the dish with celery leaves.

3 oz (85 g) button mushrooms, trimmed and sliced
1 oz (30 g) polyunsaturated margarine
2 celery stalks, sliced
1 clove garlic, crushed
1 medium onion, grated
1 tbsp wholemeal flour
14-oz (300-g) tin chopped tomatoes
10 oz (280 g) wholemeal breadcrumbs
4 oz (115 g) ground walnuts
1 egg
1 tsp chopped basil
1 tsp chopped oregano
1 tbsp chopped parsley
salt and freshly ground black pepper
4 oz (115 g) broccoli spears, cooked

Sauce
2 oz (60 g) mushrooms, trimmed and chopped
1 tbsp wholemeal flour
4 oz (100 ml) vegetable stock
4 fl oz (115 ml) skimmed milk

Garnish
celery leaves

NUTRITION FACTS	
Amount per Serving	
Calories 312	Calories from Fat 190
	% Daily Value
Total Fat 21g	32%
Saturated Fat 3g	15%
Polyunsaturated Fat 12g	0%
Monounsaturated Fat 5g	0%
Cholesterol 60mg	20%
Sodium 282mg	12%
Total Carbohydrate 22g	7%
Dietary Fibre 7g	28%
Sugars 6g	0%
Protein 11g	0%

Percent daily values are based on a 2000 calorie diet

SPICED CARROTS AND CORN WITH BREADCRUMB TOPPING

SERVES 4

An unusual blend of vegetables and spices with a crunchy topping, this is a dish to prepare now and bake later.

1 lb (450 g) carrots, scraped and
thinly sliced

salt

7-oz (160 g) tin corn

1 tbsp clear honey

½ tsp ground ginger

large pinch grated nutmeg

3 tbsp vegetable stock

2 tbsp chopped mint

pepper

oil, for brushing

Topping

4 tbsp wholemeal breadcrumbs

1 tbsp sesame seeds

1 tbsp sunflower seeds

1 oz (30 g) wholemeal flour

5 tbsp sunflower oil

salt and freshly ground black pepper

NUTRITION FACTS

Amount per Serving (ie 1 tbsp)

Calories 311	Calories from Fat 170
	% Daily Value
Total Fat 19g	29%
Saturated Fat 2g	10%
Polyunsaturated Fat 11g	0%
Monounsaturated Fat 4g	0%
Cholesterol 0mg	0%
Sodium 202mg	8%
Total Carbohydrate 33g	11%
Dietary Fibre 6g	24%
Sugars 17g	0%
Protein 5g	0%

Percent daily values are based on a 2000 calorie diet

≈ Set the oven to 190°C/375°F/Gas 5. Steam the carrots over boiling, salted water for 8–10 minutes, until they are just tender. Mix them with the corn, honey, ginger, nutmeg, stock and mint, and season with salt and pepper.

≈ Lightly brush a medium-sized ovenproof dish with oil. Spoon in the vegetable mixture, and level the top.

≈ Mix together the breadcrumbs, seeds, and flour, and gradually pour on the oil, stirring. Season the mixture with salt and pepper, and spread it over the vegetable layer. Bake the dish in the oven for 20 minutes until the topping is golden brown. Serve hot.

CHINESE MUSTARD GREENS WITH FUSILLI

SERVES 4

This quick-to-prepare, nutritious dish is perfect for a light lunch when entertaining friends.

1 lb (450 g) dried fusilli (small twists)

dash of olive oil

3 tbsp sesame oil

3 cloves of garlic, crushed

2 carrots, peeled and cut into ribbons

8 spring onions, stalks removed and
leaves shredded

5–6 tbsp dark soy sauce

3 tbsp toasted sesame seeds

≈ Bring a large saucepan of water to a boil, and add the fusilli with a dash of olive oil. Cook for about 10 minutes, stirring occasionally, until the pasta is tender. Drain thoroughly, and set aside.

≈ To cut the carrots into wafer-thin ribbons, peel away the outside skin using a vegetable peeler, then continue peeling the carrot.

≈ Heat the sesame oil in a wok or large skillet, and add the garlic. Stir-fry for 30 seconds, then add the carrot ribbons. Continue to cook for 3–4 minutes, then add the shredded spring onions. Cook for 2–3 minutes, stirring continuously.

≈ Stir in the soy sauce, sesame seeds, and the fusilli. Cook for a further 2 minutes, and serve immediately.

NUTRITION FACTS	
Amount per Serving	
Calories 465	Calories from Fat 153
	% Daily Value
Total Fat 17g	26%
Saturated Fat 2g	10%
Polyunsaturated Fat 7g	0%
Monounsaturated Fat 7g	0%
Cholesterol 0mg	0%
Sodium 17mg	0.7%
Total Carbohydrate 70g	23%
Dietary Fibre 6.5g	26%
Sugars 7g	0%
Protein 13g	0%

Percent daily values are based on a 2000 calorie diet

TUNISIAN-STYLE VEGETABLE COUSCOUS

SERVES 4

A prominent feature of North African cooking, couscous is made from particles of hard durum wheat semolina. To pre-cook couscous grains, wash them thoroughly and steam uncovered over a bowl of fast-boiling water for 30 minutes. Spread the couscous on a plate, and sprinkle with cold water before continuing to cook it in this Tunisian-style recipe.

4 oz (115 g) chickpeas, soaked
    overnight and drained

4 oz (115 g) adzuki beans, soaked
    overnight and drained

2 cloves garlic, crushed

2 leeks, sliced

2 carrots, thinly sliced

14 oz (400 g) cauliflower florets

3 courgettes, sliced

1 parsnip, thinly sliced

2 tbsp tomato purée

2 tsp ground coriander

½ tsp ground turmeric

1 tsp mixed dry herbs

1 pt (½ l) water

1 green sweet pepper, seeded, cored
    and sliced

12 oz (340 g) tomatoes, skinned and
    quartered

4 oz (115 g) dry grains (to yield 8 oz
    (225 g) pre-cooked couscous);
    (see above)

2 tbsp low-fat yogurt

salt and paprika

Garnish

fresh parsley

NUTRITION FACTS

Amount per Serving

Calories 328	Calories from Fat 27
	% Daily Value
Total Fat 3g	5%
Saturated Fat 0.5g	2.5%
Polyunsaturated Fat 1.5g	0%
Monounsaturated Fat 0.5g	0%
Cholesterol 0mg	0%
Sodium 51mg	2%
Total Carbohydrate 62g	21%
Dietary Fibre 11g	44%
Sugars 12g	0%
Protein 17g	0%

Percent daily values are based on a 2000 calorie diet

≈ Place the drained chickpeas and adzuki beans in separate saucepans, cover with water, and boil rapidly for 10 minutes. Cover and simmer for 30–40 minutes.

≈ Place the garlic, leeks, carrots, cauliflower, courgettes, parsnip, tomato purée, coriander, turmeric and herbs in a large saucepan. Add water, bring to a boil, then cover and simmer for 20 minutes.

≈ Add the garbanzo beans, adzuki beans, green pepper, and tomatoes to the vegetables. Return to a boil.

≈ Place the partly-cooked couscous in a steamer lined with a double thickness of cheesecloth, or a clean dishtowel and place over the pan of vegetables. Cover and cook for 15 minutes, stirring the grains once or twice.

≈ Stir the low-fat yogurt into the couscous, and put in a heated serving dish. Season and garnish the vegetables and serve them in another heated dish.

PEPPERS WITH APRICOT AND HAZELNUT FILLING

SERVES 4

This is a good main dish to offer a vegetarian guest. The colourful peppers have visual appeal, and the apricot and hazelnut filling provides fibre, protein and vitamins.

≈ Set the oven to 190°C/375°F/Gas 5. Place the bulgur wheat in a bowl, pour over ½ pint (¼ litre) boiling water, and leave to stand for about 15 minutes.

≈ Place the peppers in a shallow, lightly oiled dish. Heat 1 tablespoon oil in a saucepan, and fry the onion over medium heat for about 3 minutes, until it is soft. Stir in the bulgur wheat,

- hazelnuts, apricots, ginger and
- cardamom. Cook for 1 minute longer,
- stirring continuously. Add the coriander
- and yogurt, mix well and remove from
- the heat.
- ≈ Pile the filling into the pepper shells.
- Cover the dish with foil and bake in the
- oven for 30–35 minutes. Garnish with
- coriander leaves to serve.

7 oz (200 g) bulgur wheat

2 red peppers, cut in half
lengthways, seeded and cored

2 yellow peppers, cut in half
lengthwise, seeded and cored

1 tbsp sunflower oil, plus extra for
brushing

1 medium onion, chopped

1½ oz (40 g) hazelnuts, chopped

4 oz (115 g) dried apricots, chopped

½ tsp ground ginger

1 tsp ground cardamom

2 tbsp chopped coriander

3 tbsp plain low-fat yogurt

Garnish

fresh coriander

NUTRITION FACTS	
Amount per Serving	
Calories 353	Calories from Fat 90
	% Daily Value
Total Fat 10g	15%
Saturated Fat 1g	5%
Polyunsaturated Fat 2.5g	0%
Monounsaturated Fat 5g	0%
Cholesterol 1mg	0.3%
Sodium 50mg	2%
Total Carbohydrate 59g	20%
Dietary Fibre 9g	36%
Sugars 30g	0%
Protein 10g	0%

Percent daily values are based on a 2000 calorie diet

COURGETTE RAGOUT

SERVES 4

This is a good way of turning courgettes into a delicious tea-time dish or vegetarian meal. Making your own bouquet garni is important – it is better to change the herbs according to availability than to compromise with a ready-made selection.

3 tbsp olive oil

2 onions, chopped

4 celery sticks, chopped

2 carrots, diced

2 garlic cloves, crushed

1 bouquet garni

4 tbsp tomato purée

14-oz (400-g) tinned chopped tomatoes

salt and freshly ground black pepper

1½ lb (675 g) courgettes, peeled, seeded and thickly sliced

3 oz (85 g) fresh wholemeal breadcrumbs

2 tbsp chopped parsley

3 oz (85 g) low-fat hard cheese, grated

≈ Heat the oil in an ovenproof casserole. Add the onions, celery, carrots, garlic and bouquet garni. Stir well until sizzling, then cover and cook over medium heat for 20 minutes, stirring once.

≈ Stir in the tomato purée and tinned tomatoes with plenty of seasoning. Bring to a boil. Add the courgettes and mix well. Reduce the heat so that the mixture barely simmers, cover and cook very gently for 1 hour, stirring occasionally. The courgettes should be tender but not mushy.

≈ Set the oven at 205°C/400°F/Gas 6.

≈ Mix the breadcrumbs, cheese and parsley, then sprinkle the mixture over the courgettes. Bake for 20–30 minutes, until crisp and golden on top, then serve at once. If preferred, the topping may be cooked under a grill heated to a medium setting, until crisp and golden-brown.

NUTRITION FACTS	
Amount per Serving	
Calories 232	Calories from Fat 108
	% Daily Value
Total Fat 12g	18%
Saturated Fat 3g	15%
Polyunsaturated Fat 1g	0%
Monounsaturated Fat 7g	0%
Cholesterol 8mg	3%
Sodium 320mg	13%
Total Carbohydrate 21g	7%
Dietary Fibre 6g	24%
Sugars 12g	0%
Protein 11g	0%

Percent daily values are based on a 2000 calorie diet

FIVE VEGETABLE BHAJI WITH MINT

SERVES 4

Traditionally Indian, a bhaji is a spiced vegetable dish. This one is fun because every time it is cooked it has a new taste – as the combination of the five vegetables is somehow never quite the same.

¼ lb (115 g) green beans

6 oz (180 g) potatoes

¼ lb (115 g) carrots

6 oz (180 g) aubergine

¼ lb (115 g) tomatoes

1–2 green chilli peppers

2 tbsp oil

7–8 cloves garlic, finely chopped

½ tsp chilli powder

¼ tsp ground turmeric

½–¾ tsp salt

2–3 tbsp mint or coriander leaves

NUTRITION FACTS

Amount per Serving

Calories 113	Calories from Fat 54
	% Daily Value
Total Fat 6g	9%
Saturated Fat 1g	5%
Polyunsaturated Fat 4g	0%
Monounsaturated Fat 1g	0%
Cholesterol 0mg	0%
Sodium 13mg	0.5%
Total Carbohydrate 13g	0.5%
Dietary Fibre 4g	16%
Sugars 4g	0%
Protein 3g	0%

Percent daily values are based on a 2000 calorie diet

≈ Top and tail and string the beans, then chop them into bite-size pieces.

≈ Cut the potatoes into quarters and halve them again, preferably leaving the skin on.

≈ Scrape and dice the carrots.

≈ Cut the aubergine into four strips lengthways and then slice across into ½-in (1.5-cm) chunks.

≈ Roughly chop the tomatoes and green chillies.

≈ Measure the oil into a medium-sized heavy-bottomed saucepan over a medium heat. Add the garlic, stirring it as soon as it begins to turn translucent, then add all the vegetables. Also stir in the chilli powder, turmeric and salt. Mix the spices together thoroughly.

≈ Lower the heat, cover the pan and cook for another 20–25 minutes.

≈ Add the mint or coriander leaves, stir, and switch the heat off. Let stand for 2–3 minutes before serving.

GINGER AND GARLIC EGG AND PEA CURRY

SERVES 4

4 large eggs

2 tbsp oil

3 oz (85 g) chopped onion

¼ tsp cumin seeds

2 tsp ginger and garlic paste (from Asian stores)

½ tsp chilli powder

¼ tsp turmeric

½ tsp ground coriander

salt to taste

¼ tsp garam masala (available from Asian stores)

3 oz (85 g) chopped tomato

8 oz (225 g) fresh or frozen peas

1 green chilli pepper, slit

2 tbsp coriander leaves

≈ Hard-boil the eggs, remove their shells, then set aside.

≈ Heat the oil in a medium-sized heavy-bottomed saucepan and fry the onion and cumin seeds until the onion is light gold in colour.

≈ Add the ginger and garlic paste, chilli powder, turmeric, ground coriander, salt, and garam masala, and fry this mixture well for a couple of minutes, adding, whenever needed, 1 tablespoon of water, to prevent burning or sticking.

≈ Add the whole eggs and tomato, stir gently and cook for a minute.

≈ Add 1¼ cups of water and let it come to a boil before adding the peas and green chilli. Cook for another 5 minutes.

≈ Stir in the coriander leaves and remove the pan from the heat.

NUTRITION FACTS	
Amount per Serving	
Calories 150	Calories from Fat 108
	% Daily Value
Total Fat 12g	18%
Saturated Fat 2.5g	12.5%
Polyunsaturated Fat 4g	0%
Monounsaturated Fat 4g	0%
Cholesterol 238mg	79%
Sodium 90mg	3%
Total Carbohydrate 3g	1%
Dietary Fibre 1g	4%
Sugars 2g	0%
Protein 8g	0%

Percent daily values are based on a 2000 calorie diet

OKRA WITH CHILLI PEPPERS

SERVES 4

1 lb (450 g) okra

2 tbsp sunflower oil

1 large onion, thinly sliced

4 green chilli peppers, seeded and
    sliced

1 green sweet pepper, seeded and
    sliced

6 oz (180 g) tomatoes, peeled,
    seeded and chopped

salt and freshly ground black pepper

3 tbsp water

plain yogurt, to serve

NUTRITION FACTS

Amount per Serving

Calories 128	Calories from Fat 63
	% Daily Value
Total Fat 7g	11%
Saturated Fat 1g	5%
Polyunsaturated Fat 4g	0%
Monounsaturated Fat 1.5g	0%
Cholesterol 2mg	0.6%
Sodium 47mg	2%
Total Carbohydrate 10g	3%
Dietary Fibre 8g	32%
Sugars 9g	0%
Protein 6g	0%

Percent daily values are based on a 2000 calorie diet

≈ Trim the okra and prick a few times with a fork.

≈ Heat the oil in a pan and sauté the onion and chilli peppers for 5 minutes, or until softened. Add the green pepper and cook for a further 2 minutes.

≈ Stir in the chopped tomatoes, the okra and water with seasoning to taste and bring to a boil. Reduce the heat, cover the pan and simmer for 8 minutes, or until the okra is tender. Serve immediately topped with yogurt.

POTATO AND TOMATO PIE

SERVES 4

Two favourite vegetables are brought together in this simple yet tasty recipe from Portugal. It makes a good supper or lunch dish, or a vegetarian main course, and is a useful way of using leftover cooked potatoes.

≈ To make the red sweet pepper paste stir together the peppers and salt; then leave, uncovered, at room temperature for 24 hours.

≈ Preheat the grill. Rinse the sweet peppers well, drain and pat dry. Place, skin side up, on a baking sheet. Grill until the skins are charred and blistered. Leave to cool slightly before peeling off the skins and discarding.

≈ Purée the garlic and sweet peppers in a blender, pouring in the oil slowly.

≈ Preheat the oven to 205°C/400°F/ Gas 6.

≈ Lay the potato slices in a well-oiled, shallow baking dish. Spread thinly with red sweet pepper paste.

≈ Chop the parsley, garlic and chilli pepper together and mix with the oil. Add lemon juice and seasoning to taste and spread half over the potatoes.

≈ Cover with the tomatoes and spoon over the remaining parsley mixture. Trickle a little oil over the vegetables and bake for 30–40 minutes. Serve warm, not straight from the oven.

about 6 boiled or steamed medium-sized potatoes, thinly sliced

Red Sweet Pepper Paste (see below), for spreading

1 bunch of parsley

1 garlic clove

1 fresh red chilli pepper, seeded

3 tbsp virgin oil, plus extra for trickling

squeeze of lemon juice

salt and pepper

1¼ lb (565 g) well-flavoured tomatoes, skinned, seeded and sliced

Red Sweet Pepper Paste

3 large red sweet peppers, seeded and quartered lengthwise

1 tbsp sea salt

2 garlic cloves

2 tbsp olive oil

NUTRITION FACTS	
Amount per Serving	
Calories 236	Calories from Fat 135
	% Daily Value
Total Fat 15g	23%
Saturated Fat 2g	10%
Polyunsaturated Fat 2g	0%
Monounsaturated Fat 10g	0%
Cholesterol 0mg	0%
Sodium 22mg	1%
Total Carbohydrate 24g	8%
Dietary Fibre 6g	24%
Sugars 13g	0%
Protein 4g	0%

Percent daily values are based on a 2000 calorie diet

AUBERGINE WITH SPICY POTATOES

SERVES 4

¾ lb (340 g) aubergine

½ lb (225 g) potatoes

2 tbsp oil

3 oz (85 g) sliced onion

½ tsp cumin seeds

½ tsp roasted and crushed coriander
    seeds

½ tsp curry powder (optional)

1 tsp grated ginger root

4–5 cloves garlic, finely chopped

½ tsp chilli powder

¼ tsp turmeric

salt to taste

1 tbsp low-fat plain yogurt

½ tsp sugar

1–2 green chilli peppers, chopped

3 oz (85 g) chopped tomato

1 tbsp lemon juice

2 tbsp chopped coriander leaves

≈ Wash the aubergine. Cut it into quarters lengthwise, then, holding the pieces together, cut them across into ½-in (1.5-cm) chunks.

≈ Scrub the potatoes thoroughly and do not peel them, then cut each one into quarters and each quarter twice or more so that you have at least twelve bite-sized pieces from each potato.

≈ Heat the oil in a medium-sized heavy-bottomed saucepan and fry the onion until it turns light brown.

≈ Add the cumin and coriander seeds and the curry leaves, if using. Fry these for a minute or so, then add the ginger, half the garlic, the chili powder, turmeric and salt. Cook this mixture over quite a high heat, adding 2 tablespoons of water as necessary so that the spice paste deepens in colour and does not stick. This should not take longer than 2 minutes.

≈ Add the aubergine, then the yogurt, sugar and green chilli peppers. Mix everything together and cook for 2 to 3 minutes. Add 5⅓ fl oz (150 ml) of water, lower the heat and simmer for 15 minutes, with the lid firmly on.

≈ Add the potato, chilli peppers and tomato. Ensuring that the lid is firmly on, simmer for another 10 minutes, checking it occasionally to make sure that it is not sticking or burning. If it seems a bit too dry or you would prefer a little more sauce, just add a little more water and let it simmer for a few more minutes.

≈ Lastly, add the remaining garlic, the lemon juice and coriander leaves. Cook for 1 more minute, gently stir to mix it thoroughly, then turn off the heat.

NUTRITION FACTS	
Amount per Serving	
Calories 125	Calories from Fat 54
	% Daily Value
Total Fat 6g	9%
Saturated Fat 1g	5%
Polyunsaturated Fat 4g	0%
Monounsaturated Fat 1g	0%
Cholesterol 0mg	0%
Sodium 15mg	0.6%
Total Carbohydrate 15.5g	5%
Dietary Fibre 4g	16%
Sugars 5g	0%
Protein 3g	0%

Percent daily values are based on a 2000 calorie diet

132

COURGETTE AND SWEETCORN CRUNCH

SERVES 4

Semolina and cheese topping adds a pleasing crunch to this dish.

1½ lb (675 g) courgettes, peeled,
    seeded and thickly sliced

1 small onion, finely chopped

1 tsp ground mace

salt and freshly ground black pepper

1 bouquet garni

2 tsp olive oil

12-oz (340-g) tin sweetcorn, drained

4 oz (115 g) walnuts, chopped

2 tbsp semolina

4 tbsp grated low-fat hard cheese

4 tbsp dry white breadcrumbs

NUTRITION FACTS	
Amount per Serving	
Calories 312	Calories from Fat 190
	% Daily Value
Total Fat 21g	32%
Saturated Fat 3g	15%
Polyunsaturated Fat 12g	0%
Monounsaturated Fat 5g	0%
Cholesterol 4mg	1%
Sodium 1098mg	46%
Total Carbohydrate 19g	6%
Dietary Fibre 5g	20%
Sugars 6g	0%
Protein 12g	0%

Percent daily values are based on a 2000 calorie diet

≈ Place the courgettes, onion and seasoning in a large ovenproof casserole and mix well. Add the bouquet garni and the oil and mix again to coat the vegetables. Heat until the mixture begins to sizzle, then put a tight-fitting lid on the pan and cook gently for 25 minutes. Regulate the heat so that the mixture just murmurs in the pan.

≈ Add the sweetcorn, mix well and cook for 5 minutes, covered. The courgettes should be tender but firm.

≈ Mix the nuts, semolina, low-fat cheese and breadcrumbs, then sprinkle the mixture over the vegetables and put under a moderately hot grill until evenly browned. If the mixture is browned too quickly it will become dark or burn – a lower heat is more successful. Serve straight away.

THAI NOODLES WITH CHILLI PEPPERS AND VEGETABLES

SERVES 4

Rice or noodles, whether boiled or fried, form the basis of most meals in Thailand. Thai cooking is often slightly perfumed by the lemon grass which features strongly in many dishes.

6 oz (180 g) thin vermicelli

2 tbsp sunflower oil

2 lemon grass stalks, outer leaves removed and chopped

1-inch (2.5 cm) piece root ginger, peeled and grated

1 red onion, cut into thin wedges

2 garlic cloves, crushed

4 red Thai chilli peppers, seeded and sliced

1 red sweet pepper, seeded and cut into matchsticks

4 oz (115 g) carrot, very thinly sliced with a vegetable peeler

4 oz (115 g) courgettes, trimmed and sliced with a vegetable peeler

3 oz (85 g) mange tout, trimmed and cut diagonally in half

6 spring onions, trimmed and diagonally sliced

4 oz (115 g) cashew nuts

2 tbsp soy sauce

juice of 1 orange

1 tsp clear honey

1 tbsp sesame oil

≈ Cook the noodles in lightly salted boiling water for 3 minutes. Drain, plunge into cold water, then drain again and reserve.

≈ Heat the oil in a wok or large pan and stir-fry the lemon grass and ginger for 2 minutes. Discard the lemon grass and ginger, keeping the oil in the pan.

· ≈ Add the onion, garlic and chilli peppers, and stir-fry for 2 minutes. Add the red sweet pepper and cook for a further 2 minutes. Add the remaining vegetables and stir-fry for 2 minutes.
· Then add the reserved noodles and cashew nuts with the soy sauce, orange juice and honey. Stir-fry for 1 minute.
· Add the sesame oil and stir-fry for 30 seconds. Serve immediately.

NUTRITION FACTS	
Amount per Serving	
Calories 439	Calories from Fat 211

	% Daily Value
Total Fat 23.5g	36%
Saturated Fat 3.5g	17%
Polyunsaturated Fat 7g	0%
Monounsaturated Fat 9g	0%
Cholesterol 0mg	0%
Sodium 194mg	8%
Total Carbohydrate 48g	16%
Dietary Fibre 6g	24%
Sugars 11g	0%
Protein 12g	0%

Percent daily values are based on a 2000 calorie diet

VEGETABLE MEDLEY

SERVES 4

This is a delicious sauce. Serve the mixed vegetables with shells, spirals or pasta shapes rather than with long, thin pasta.

6 oz (180 g) cauliflower, broken into small florets

salt and freshly ground black pepper

2 tbsp olive oil

2 tbsp butter

1 onion, chopped

6 oz (180 g) baby carrots, quartered lengthways and thinly sliced

8 oz (225 g) young courgettes, very lightly peeled and thinly sliced

8 oz (225 g) sliced button mushrooms

1 large, leafy sprig of tarragon, chopped

grated rind of ½ a lemon

squeeze of lemon juice

NUTRITION FACTS	
Amount per Serving	
Calories 134	Calories from Fat 100
	% Daily Value
Total Fat 11g	17%
Saturated Fat 4g	20%
Polyunsaturated Fat 1g	0%
Monounsaturated Fat 5g	0%
Cholesterol 12mg	4%
Sodium 62mg	2.5%
Total Carbohydrate 6g	2%
Dietary Fibre 4g	16%
Sugars 5g	0%
Protein 4g	0%

Percent daily values are based on a 2000 calorie diet

≈ Cook the cauliflower in boiling salted water for about 3 minutes, until lightly cooked. Drain well.

≈ Heat the olive oil and butter in a large saucepan. Add the onion, carrots and cauliflower, and stir well; then cover the pan and cook for 10 minutes. Shake the pan occasionally to prevent the vegetables sticking.

≈ Add the courgettes, mushrooms, tarragon, lemon rind and juice. Stir well, cover the pan again, and cook for a further 2–3 minutes, or until the courgettes are bright green and tender, but with a bit of bite and full of flavour. Taste for seasoning before serving.

136

ARMENIAN VEGETABLE STEW

SERVES 4

There are no hard and fast rules to making this Armenian specialty. It can incorporate whatever is in the refrigerator – for example, substitute turnip for carrots, cabbage for celery. It can be served as a main course or as a side dish.

≈ Preheat the oven to 180°C/350°F/ Gas 4. Place the oil in a large enamelled or stainless steel casserole and warm it over medium heat. Add the garlic and stir to flavour the oil, about 2 minutes. Pour in the stock and add the bay leaf, herbs and seasoning to taste. Bring to a boil.

≈ Add the vegetables, little by little, stirring to combine as you add them. Cover the casserole with a lid or foil, and transfer to the oven. Bake for about 1 hour or until the vegetables are all tender, stirring occasionally.

3 fl oz (85 ml) olive oil

4 cloves garlic, crushed

8 fl oz (200 ml) vegetable stock

1 bay leaf

½ tsp dried tarragon

½ tsp dried oregano

salt and freshly ground black pepper

2 medium carrots, halved and thinly sliced

4 oz (115 g) fresh stringless green beans, cut into ½ in (1.5 cm) lengths

2 small potatoes, peeled and diced

2 celery stalks, halved lengthways and thinly sliced

1 courgette, thinly sliced into rounds

1 small aubergine, halved and thinly sliced

1 small red onion, thinly sliced

1 small cauliflower, broken into florets

½ red sweet pepper, cored, seeded and cut into strips

½ green sweet pepper, cored, seeded and cut into strips

4 oz (115 g) shelled fresh peas

NUTRITION FACTS	
Amount per Serving	
Calories 295	Calories from Fat 216
	% Daily Value
Total Fat 24g	37%
Saturated Fat 3.5g	17.5%
Polyunsaturated Fat 3g	0%
Monounsaturated Fat 16.5g	0%
Cholesterol 0mg	0%
Sodium 26mg	1%
Total Carbohydrate 15g	5%
Dietary Fibre 8g	32%
Sugars 9g	0%
Protein 6g	0%

Percent daily values are based on a 2000 calorie diet

SIDE DISHES

ARTICHOKES WITH TOMATO SAUCE

SERVES 4

4 large artichokes

1–2 tbsp oil

1 large onion, chopped

2 cloves garlic, chopped

425 g/15-oz can tomatoes

1 tbsp tomato paste

2 tsp fresh oregano, chopped

lemon juice

salt and freshly ground black pepper

≈ Rinse the artichokes thoroughly under cold water and leave them upside down to drain. Bring a very large pan of salted water to the boil, put the artichokes in and boil vigorously for 30–50 minutes, depending on the size. When an outer leaf comes away at a gentle tug, the artichokes are ready.

≈ Meanwhile, make the sauce. Heat the oil in a pan and fry the onion and garlic until transparent. Add the tomatoes, tomato paste and oregano and reduce until the sauce is of pouring consistency but not sloppy. Season with salt and pepper and a dash of lemon juice to taste.

≈ Drain the artichokes. When cool, pull out the tiny inner leaves together with the hairy inedible choke. Spoon in some tomato sauce. Stand each artichoke in a pool of sauce on an individual dish and serve.

NUTRITION FACTS	
Amount per Serving	
Calories 92	Calories from Fat 45
	% Daily Value
Total Fat 5g	8%
Saturated Fat 1g	5%
Polyunsaturated Fat 0.5g	0%
Monounsaturated Fat 3g	0%
Cholesterol 0mg	0%
Sodium 54mg	2%
Total Carbohydrate 12g	4%
Dietary Fibre 4.5g	18%
Sugars 6g	0%
Protein 3g	0%

Percent daily values are based on a 2000 calorie diet

PASTA WITH PEPPER SAUCE AND OLIVES

SERVES 4

This low-fat Pepper Sauce helps to keep the calories in this dish down.

350 g/12 oz dried rigatoni (short tubes)

dash of olive oil

50 g/2 oz pitted black olives, chopped

grated cheese, to serve

Pepper Sauce

2 red peppers

4 cloves of garlic, peeled

300 ml/10 fl oz vegetable stock

salt and freshly ground black pepper

≈ Bring a large saucepan of water to the boil and add the rigatoni with a dash of olive oil. Cook for about 10 minutes, stirring occasionally, until tender. Drain and return to the saucepan. Set aside.

≈ Skin, de-seed and chop the peppers.

≈ To make the sauce, place the chopped pepper, garlic and vegetable stock in a food processor or blender, and season with salt and freshly ground black pepper. Purée until smooth.

≈ Stir the Pepper Sauce into the rigatoni with the chopped olives. Serve with grated cheese.

NUTRITION FACTS	
Amount per Serving	
Calories 487	Calories from Fat 72
	% Daily Value
Total Fat 8g	12%
Saturated Fat 3g	15%
Polyunsaturated Fat 1.5g	0%
Monounsaturated Fat 3g	0%
Cholesterol 10mg	3%
Sodium 336mg	14%
Total Carbohydrate 92g	31%
Dietary Fibre 7g	28%
Sugars 8g	0%
Protein 17g	0%

Percent daily values are based on a 2000 calorie diet

ROAST POTATOES IN SWEET HOT SAUCE

SERVES 4

*O*riginating as Spanish peasant fare, called Patatas Bravas, *it is easy to see why this simple dish is so popular.*

1 onion, chopped

2 tbsp olive oil

1 bay leaf

2 red chilli peppers

2 tsp garlic

1 tbsp tomato paste

½ tbsp sugar (up to 1 tbsp, if the sauce is too tart for your liking)

1 tbsp soy sauce

425 g/15-oz can plum tomatoes, chopped

1 glass of white wine

salt and black pepper

8 medium potatoes

≈ To prepare the sauce, sweat the onions in the oil with the bay leaf. When soft, add the chilli peppers, garlic, tomato paste, sugar and soy sauce. Sweat for a further 5 minutes on a low heat.

≈ Add the chopped tomatoes and white wine. Stir and bring to the boil. Simmer for 10 minutes. Taste and season.

≈ This sauce should be slightly sweet; the flavour of the tomatoes should not dominate it.

≈ Cut the potatoes into chunks.

≈ Grease a baking tray. Season the potatoes well and brush with oil.

≈ Roast in a hot oven, 230°C/450°F/Gas Mark 8, until golden.

≈ Pour the tomato sauce over the potatoes and serve.

NUTRITION FACTS

Amount per Serving

Calories 254	Calories from Fat 54
	% Daily Value
Total Fat 6g	9%
Saturated Fat 1g	5%
Polyunsaturated Fat 1g	0%
Monounsaturated Fat 4g	0%
Cholesterol 0mg	0%
Sodium 70mg	3%
Total Carbohydrate 41g	14%
Dietary Fibre 5g	20%
Sugars 7g	0%
Protein 6g	0%

Percent daily values are based on a 2000 calorie diet

COURGETTES WITH DILL

SERVES 4

This delicious vegetable dish could not be simpler to make. It's an ideal accompaniment to any main dish.

50 ml/2 fl oz olive oil

1 onion, chopped

1 tsp crushed garlic

450 g/1 lb courgettes, topped, tailed, and sliced in thickish rounds

½ tsp black pepper

2 tsp paprika

1 tbsp dill, chopped (not the stalks)

150 ml/5 fl oz soured cream

salt to taste

≈ Heat oil in a large pan. Cook the onion and garlic gently until soft. Turn up the heat.

≈ Add the courgettes, garlic and black pepper and toss.

≈ Cook for 5–10 minutes, stirring to cook both sides of the courgette slices.

≈ When brown, add the paprika, dill, and soured cream. Season and serve.

NUTRITION FACTS	
Amount per Serving	
Calories 228	Calories from Fat 200
	% Daily Value
Total Fat 22g	34%
Saturated Fat 7g	35%
Polyunsaturated Fat 2g	0%
Monounsaturated Fat 12g	0%
Cholesterol 23mg	8%
Sodium 17mg	0.7%
Total Carbohydrate 5g	2%
Dietary Fibre 2g	8%
Sugars 4g	0%
Protein 3g	0%

Percent daily values are based on a 2000 calorie diet

GREEK MUSHROOMS

SERVES 6

Meze is a type of appetizer, eaten especially with an aperitif or other drink in Greece. It is best kept simple, with the use of fresh, firm mushrooms and a good-quality olive oil for the best flavour.

150 ml/5 fl oz olive oil

125 ml/4 fl oz dry white wine

salt and freshly ground black pepper, to taste

1 tsp dried thyme

3 garlic cloves, crushed

4 tbsp chopped fresh parsley

600 g/1¼ lb tiny button mushrooms, cleaned

freshly squeezed juice of 1 lemon

chopped fresh parsley, to garnish

NUTRITION FACTS	
Amount per Serving	
Calories 245	Calories from Fat 225
	% Daily Value
Total Fat 25g	38%
Saturated Fat 4g	20%
Polyunsaturated Fat 2g	0%
Monounsaturated Fat 18g	0%
Cholesterol 0mg	0%
Sodium 7mg	0.3%
Total Carbohydrate 1g	0.3%
Dietary Fibre 2g	8%
Sugars 0g	0%
Protein 2g	0%

Percent daily values are based on a 2000 calorie diet

≈ Place all the ingredients, except the mushrooms and half the lemon juice in a large saucepan and bring to the boil. Reduce the heat and stir in the mushrooms. Cover and simmer for 8–10 minutes.

≈ Transfer the mushrooms and the liquid to a serving dish and allow to cool completely. Serve at room temperature, sprinkled with the remaining lemon juice and garnished with chopped fresh parsley.

144

FRENCH PEAS WITH LETTUCE

SERVES 4

Thanks, no doubt, to the mass availability of the frozen variety, peas have become an all-too-familiar vegetable in some households. This version of the French way of cooking them gives them a culinary fillip.

≈ Blanch the peas and onions or shallots in boiling, salted water for 5 minutes, then drain.

≈ Put the peas, onions, lettuce, stock, and yogurt in a pan and season with salt and pepper. Bring to a boil, cover the pan and simmer gently for 10 minutes.

• Stir in the sugar and adjust the seasoning if necessary.

≈ Sprinkle with mint before serving.

1 kg/2¼ lb fresh peas, shelled

225 g/½ lb small onions or shallots, peeled and left whole

salt

8 outer lettuce leaves, torn into small pieces

6 tbsp vegetable stock

3 tbsp natural low-fat yogurt

black pepper

1 tsp sugar

Garnish

2 tbsp chopped mint

NUTRITION FACTS	
Amount per Serving	
Calories 246	Calories from Fat 36
	% Daily Value
Total Fat 4g	6%
Saturated Fat 1g	5%
Polyunsaturated Fat 2g	0%
Monounsaturated Fat 0.5g	0%
Cholesterol 1mg	0.3%
Sodium 20mg	0.8%
Total Carbohydrate 36g	12%
Dietary Fibre 18g	72%
Sugars 12g	0%
Protein 19g	0%

Percent daily values are based on a 2000 calorie diet

ONIONS ROASTED IN RED WINE

SERVES 4

Oven-roasted onions are an excellent complement to many main dishes.

4 large Spanish onions
2 tbsp sunflower oil
180 ml/6 fl oz red wine
300 ml/10 fl oz vegetable stock
salt and black pepper

Garnish
parsley sprigs

NUTRITION FACTS	
Amount per Serving	
Calories 120	Calories from Fat 54
	% Daily Value
Total Fat 6g	9%
Saturated Fat 1g	5%
Polyunsaturated Fat 4g	0%
Monounsaturated Fat 1g	0%
Cholesterol 0mg	0%
Sodium 6mg	0.25%
Total Carbohydrate 10g	3%
Dietary Fibre 2g	8%
Sugars 7g	0%
Protein 1.5g	0%

Percent daily values are based on a 2000 calorie diet

≈ Preheat the oven to 170°C/325°F/ Gas Mark 3. Peel the onions, and cut a thin slice from each base, so that they will stand upright.
≈ Heat the oil in a pan, and fry the onions on all sides over medium heat. Pour on the wine, bring to the boil and simmer for 2–3 minutes. Pour on the stock, season with salt and pepper, and bring back to the boil.

≈ If you have used a pan, transfer the onions and sauce to an ovenproof dish. Bake uncovered in the oven for 1¼–1½ hours until the onions are soft and the sauce has reduced and thickened. Serve hot, garnished with the parsley.

TANGY BEANS AND PASTA

SERVES 4

Use tiny pasta shapes for this delicious and nutritious dish and serve with warm, crusty French bread.

50 g/2 oz dried pastina (tiny shapes)
dash of olive oil
400 g/14-oz can mixed beans
1 red pepper
2 tsp dried oregano

Dressing
2 cloves of garlic, crushed
4 tbsp extra virgin olive oil
2–3 tbsp balsamic vinegar
1 tsp tomato paste
salt and freshly ground black pepper

NUTRITION FACTS	
Amount per Serving	
Calories 273	Calories from Fat 117
	% Daily Value
Total Fat 13g	20%
Saturated Fat 2g	10%
Polyunsaturated Fat 1.5g	0%
Monounsaturated Fat 9g	0%
Cholesterol 0mg	0%
Sodium 409mg	17%
Total Carbohydrate 30g	10%
Dietary Fibre 9g	36%
Sugars 6.5g	0%
Protein 10g	0%

Percent daily values are based on a 2000 calorie diet

≈ Bring a large saucepan of water to the boil and add the pastina with a dash of olive oil. Cook for about 8 minutes, stirring occasionally, until tender. Drain, and rinse under cold running water. Drain again, and place in a large mixing bowl.

≈ Deseed and chop the pepper. Add the beans, pepper and oregano to the pasta.
≈ Place all the dressing ingredients in a screw-top jar, and shake well to combine. Pour the dressing over the mixture, toss, and chill for at least 30 minutes before serving.

MUSHROOM, PEAR, GREEN BEAN AND WALNUT SALAD

SERVES 6

This mixed fruit, vegetable, and nut salad, with its sweet-and-sour dressing, makes a substantial accompaniment to a plain dish but can also be served alone as a first course.

¼ lb (115 g) green beans, trimmed and halved

2 ripe pears, peeled, cored, and sliced

2 tsp lemon juice

½ lb (225 g) button mushrooms, trimmed, halved or sliced

1 small bibb lettuce, washed, and drained and torn into small pieces

3 oz (85 g) walnut halves

Dressing

1 tbsp sunflower oil

3 tbsp plain low-fat yogurt

1 tbsp clear honey

salt and freshly ground black pepper

NUTRITION FACTS	
Amount per Serving	
Calories 131	Calories from Fat 72
	% Daily Value
Total Fat 8g	12%
Saturated Fat 1g	5%
Polyunsaturated Fat 5g	0%
Monounsaturated Fat 1g	0%
Cholesterol 1mg	0.3%
Sodium 18mg	0.75%
Total Carbohydrate 12g	4%
Dietary Fibre 3.5g	14%
Sugars 12g	0%
Protein 3g	0%

Percent daily values are based on a 2000 calorie diet

≈ Cook the green beans in boiling water for 2 minutes, then drain them in a colander. Run cold water through them to prevent further cooking, then drain again.

≈ Sprinkle the pear slices with the lemon juice, then toss them in a bowl with the beans, mushroom, lettuce and walnuts.

≈ Mix the dressing ingredients, pour over the salad, and toss thoroughly.

Serve.

HOT BEETROOT IN YOGURT AND MUSTARD SAUCE

SERVES 4

A popular salad vegetable in many countries, beetroot has an equally attractive role to play as a hot vegetable accompaniment. This dish has middle-European origins.

1 lb (450 g) small beetroot, trimmed
and scrubbed

salt

6 oz (180 g) low-fat yogurt

1 tsp cornflour

2 tsp wholegrain mustard

1 clove garlic, crushed

1 tbsp chopped mint

freshly ground black pepper

Garnish

2 spring onions, trimmed and thinly
sliced

≈ Cook the beetroot in boiling salted water for 30 minutes, or until they are tender. Drain them and, as soon as they are cool enough to handle, scrape them. If the vegetables are very small, they are best left whole; others may be sliced or diced.

≈ Mix the yogurt with the cornflour, and put in a pan with the mustard and garlic. Heat gently, then stir in the beetroot. When they have heated through, stir in the mint and season with pepper. Serve warm, garnished with the spring onion slices.

NUTRITION FACTS	
Amount per Serving	
Calories 76	Calories from Fat 9
	% Daily Value
Total Fat 1g	1.5%
Saturated Fat 0.2g	1%
Polyunsaturated Fat 0.2g	0%
Monounsaturated Fat 0.3g	0%
Cholesterol 2mg	0.6%
Sodium 148mg	6%
Total Carbohydrate 14g	5%
Dietary Fibre 3g	12%
Sugars 11g	0%
Protein 4g	0%

Percent daily values are based on a 2000 calorie diet

AUBERGINE DIP WITH SUNFLOWER SEEDS

SERVES 4

1 tbsp sunflower seeds

8 oz (225 g) grated aubergine

2–3 garlic cloves, crushed

pinch of salt

3–4 tbsp skimmed milk

8 oz (225 g) low-fat plain yogurt

1 tsp artificial sweetener

¼ tsp cumin seeds, crushed

¼ tsp freshly ground black pepper

3 oz (85 g) chopped tomato

few mint leaves or pinch of dried
   mint

pinch of chilli powder

NUTRITION FACTS	
Amount per Serving	
Calories 74	Calories from Fat 27
	% Daily Value
Total Fat 3g	5%
Saturated Fat 0.5g	2.5%
Polyunsaturated Fat 1g	0%
Monounsaturated Fat 0.5g	0%
Cholesterol 3mg	1%
Sodium 63mg	3%
Total Carbohydrate 8g	3%
Dietary Fibre 2g	8%
Sugars 7g	0%
Protein 5g	0%

Percent daily values are based on a 2000 calorie diet

≈ Put the sunflower seeds into a heavy-bottomed pan and heat them over a medium heat. Move the seeds around continuously with a wooden spoon, roasting them for 1 minute. Switch the heat off, but keep on stirring the seeds as the pan cools, then leave them to cool completely.

≈ Pour 4 tablespoons of water into a small saucepan, together with the aubergine, garlic and a pinch of salt, then bring it to a boil. Cook for 2 to 3 minutes, until the aubergine is softened to a pulp, then remove the pan from the heat and leave it to one side to cool.

≈ Beat the milk and yogurt together in a bowl until smooth, then add the aubergine, sugar, cumin seeds and pepper and blend well.

≈ Add the tomato and mint leaves or dried mint.

≈ Sprinkle the chilli powder over the top and garnish with the sunflower seeds just before serving.

JAPANESE-STYLE VEGETABLE TEMPURA

SERVES 6

Maximize the colour and texture of a variety of vegetables in this crisp Japanese dish. It can be served to complement baked or grilled dishes, or presented as the main dish with brown rice.

Sauce

2-in (5-cm) piece fresh root ginger, peeled and grated

2 tbsp soy sauce

1 tsp clear honey

4 fl oz (100 ml) boiling water

Vegetables

12 oz (340 g) cauliflower florets

2 large carrots, scraped and cut into julienne strips

1 large onion, sliced into rings

1 red sweet pepper, cored, seeded and sliced

4 oz (115 g) small button mushrooms, trimmed and halved

flour, for coating

sunflower oil, for deep frying

Batter

4 oz (115 g) wholemeal flour

2 tbsp fine cornmeal

2 tbsp arrowroot

1/2 pt (300 ml) water

≈ First make the sauce. Place the ginger, soy sauce and honey in an ovenproof serving bowl, pour on the boiling water, and stir well. Leave to cool.

≈ To make the batter, mix the dry ingredients in a bowl and gradually pour on the water, beating all the time.

≈ Toss all the vegetables in flour to coat them; shake off any excess. Heat the oil in a wok or deep-frying pan.

≈ Using a slotted spoon, dip the vegetables in the batter a few at a time, and allow the excess to drain back into the bowl. Fry the vegetables in several batches, reheating the oil between each one, until they are evenly golden brown.

≈ Lift out the vegetables and toss them on crumpled paper towels to drain off excess oil. Serve at once with the sauce in a separate dish.

NUTRITION FACTS	
Amount per Serving	
Calories 225	Calories from Fat 90
	% Daily Value
Total Fat 10g	15%
Saturated Fat 1g	5%
Polyunsaturated Fat 6g	0%
Monounsaturated Fat 2g	0%
Cholesterol 0mg	0%
Sodium 12mg	0.5%
Total Carbohydrate 30g	10%
Dietary Fibre 5g	20%
Sugars 6g	0%
Protein 4.5g	0%

Percent daily values are based on a 2000 calorie diet

HARICOT BEANS WITH TOMATO SAUCE AND ONION

SERVES 4

This recipe is distinguished from other beans in tomato sauce recipes by the addition of a mound of finely chopped raw onion and some chopped coriander or parsley to each portion as it is served. This really livens up the dish, but it is important to use a mild onion.

8 oz (225 g) haricot beans, soaked overnight and drained

3 tbsp virgin olive oil

3 garlic cloves, finely chopped

3 tbsp chopped parsley

1 tbsp chopped mixed thyme and rosemary

1 bay leaf

pinch of dried oregano

¼–½ tsp crushed red chilli pepper flakes

8 fl oz (225 ml) water

2 large tomatoes, peeled, seeded and diced

salt and freshly ground black pepper

¼ Spanish onion, very finely chopped

finely chopped coriander or parsley, to serve

≈ Put the beans into a saucepan and just cover with water. Boil for 10 minutes and then simmer for about 50 minutes or until the beans are tender.

≈ Heat the oil, garlic, herbs and crushed red chilli pepper gently for 4 minutes. Add the water, bring to a boil, then cover and simmer for 5 minutes. Stir in the tomatoes, cover again and simmer for 4 minutes.

≈ Drain the beans and stir into the tomato mixture gently. Season and simmer for 4–5 minutes.

≈ Ladle the beans and sauce into four warmed soup plates and put a small mound of onion and some coriander or parsley in the centre of each.

NUTRITION FACTS	
Amount per Serving	
Calories 252	Calories from Fat 80
	% Daily Value
Total Fat 9g	14%
Saturated Fat 1g	5%
Polyunsaturated Fat 1g	0%
Monounsaturated Fat 6g	0%
Cholesterol 0mg	0%
Sodium 30mg	1%
Total Carbohydrate 31g	10%
Dietary Fibre 14.5g	58%
Sugars 4g	0%
Protein 13g	0%

Percent daily values are based on a 2000 calorie diet

PAPRIKA POTATOES IN SPICY SAUCE

SERVES 6

The potatoes can be pre-cooked and left in the spicy sauce, ready to be reheated while the main dish is cooking.

2¼ lb (1 kg) potatoes, scrubbed

salt

1 tsp sunflower oil

1 medium onion, chopped

1 clove garlic, crushed

1 tbsp paprika

10 fl oz (300 ml) vegetable stock

8 oz (300 g) tin tomatoes, chopped

½ tsp caraway seeds

1 small green sweet pepper, cored, seeded and chopped

freshly ground black pepper

3 tbsp plain low-fat yogurt

Garnish

2 tbsp chopped parsley

≈ Cook the potatoes in boiling salted water for 5 minutes, then drain them. Unless they are very small, cut the potatoes into medium-sized slices.

≈ Heat the oil in a saucepan, and fry the onion and garlic over medium heat for about 3 minutes, until the onion is soft. Stir in the paprika, and cook for 1 minute. Pour on the stock, and add the tomatoes (including juice), caraway seeds and green sweet pepper. Season with salt and pepper, add the potatoes, and stir well. Bring to a boil and simmer, uncovered, for 20 minutes, until the potatoes are tender and the sauce has thickened.

≈ Stir in the yogurt, taste the sauce, and adjust the seasoning if necessary. Serve hot, sprinkled with the parsley.

NUTRITION FACTS	
Amount per Serving	
Calories 153	Calories from Fat 9
	% Daily Value
Total Fat 1g	1.5%
Saturated Fat 0.2g	1%
Polyunsaturated Fat 0.6g	0%
Monounsaturated Fat 0.2g	0%
Cholesterol 1mg	0.3%
Sodium 40mg	2%
Total Carbohydrate 33g	11%
Dietary Fibre 4g	16%
Sugars 4.5g	0%
Protein 5g	0%

Percent daily values are based on a 2000 calorie diet

1½ tbsp lemon juice

2 tbsp white-wine vinegar

1½ tbsp sunflower or olive oil

½ tsp sugar

freshly ground black pepper

1 large red onion

2½ lb (1 kg) white cabbage

6 tbsp finely shredded fresh mint

NUTRITION FACTS

Amount per Serving

Calories 89	Calories from Fat 27

	% Daily Value
Total Fat 3g	5%
Saturated Fat 0.4g	2%
Polyunsaturated Fat 0.4g	0%
Monounsaturated Fat 2g	0%
Cholesterol 0mg	0%
Sodium 15mg	0.6%
Total Carbohydrate 12g	4%
Dietary Fibre 6g	24%
Sugars 12g	0%
Protein 3g	0%

Percent daily values are based on a 2000 calorie diet

2 tbsp vegetable oil

1 onion, cut in half and thinly sliced

2 dessert apples, peeled, cored and
    thinly sliced

1 red cabbage, quartered, cored and
    shredded

4 tbsp red-wine vinegar

2 to 3 tbsp light brown sugar

4 oz (100 ml) vegetable stock or water

salt and freshly ground black pepper

NUTRITION FACTS

Amount per Serving

Calories 108	Calories from Fat 36

	% Daily Value
Total Fat 4g	6%
Saturated Fat 0.4g	2%
Polyunsaturated Fat 2.5g	0%
Monounsaturated Fat 0.5g	0%
Cholesterol 0mg	0%
Sodium 16mg	0.6%
Total Carbohydrate 17g	6%
Dietary Fibre 5g	20%
Sugars 17g	0%
Protein 2g	0%

Percent daily values are based on a 2000 calorie diet

CABBAGE AND MINT SALAD

SERVES 6

*C*abbage *is a staple of the former Soviet Union, but in the south the spicing is notably different, and sour cream gives way to yogurt, when used. This is a cool, refreshing "coleslaw" served as a* zakuska *or to accompany a picnic or outdoor meal.*

≈ Beat together the lemon juice and vinegar in a large bowl. Whisk in the oil, sugar and a generous dash of pepper. Halve and finely slice all but one-quarter of the red onion. Stir the onion slices into the dressing, and wrap the remaining section in foil. Then gently toss the shredded cabbage and mint leaves in the dressing. Combine thoroughly, and chill for at least 3 hours.

≈ Just before serving, slice the reserved onion and sprinkle over the salad.

SWEET AND SOUR RED CABBAGE

SERVES 6

*C*abbage *is an important ingredient in many kitchens, especially in Russia and Central Europe. This braised sweet-and-sour cabbage dish is also delicious served cold. If you want to make the green cabbage version, use white-wine vinegar or lemon juice and white sugar.*

≈ In a large, heavy-bottomed, non-aluminium pan, over medium-high heat, heat oil. Add onion and cook until soft and golden, 5–7 minutes. Add sliced apples and cook until they begin to brown, 2–3 minutes.

≈ Add cabbage and remaining ingredients. Simmer, covered, stirring occasionally and adding water if necessary until cabbage is tender, 30–40 minutes. Uncover and cook until liquid is absorbed. Spoon into a serving bowl.

INDIAN-STYLE VEGETABLES

SERVES 4

¼ lb (115 g) cauliflower

¼ lb (115 g) green beans

¼ lb (115 g) red and green sweet
   peppers

3 tbsp oil

3–4 whole dried chilli peppers,
   broken roughly

1 tsp cumin seeds

¼ tsp turmeric

½ tsp salt

¼ lb (115 g) carrots

3 oz (85 g) chopped tomatoes

2 tsp grated ginger root

3–4 plump cloves garlic, chopped or
   crushed

1 green chilli pepper, chopped

2–3 tbsp chopped coriander

NUTRITION FACTS	
Amount per Serving	
Calories 111	Calories from Fat 80
	% Daily Value
Total Fat 9g	14%
Saturated Fat 1g	5%
Polyunsaturated Fat 6g	0%
Monounsaturated Fat 2g	0%
Cholesterol 0mg	0%
Sodium 12mg	0.5%
Total Carbohydrate 6g	2%
Dietary Fibre 3g	12%
Sugars 5g	0%
Protein 2g	0%

Percent daily values are based on a 2000 calorie diet

≈ Cut the cauliflower into small florets.

≈ Trim the green beans and cut each one into 3–4 pieces.

≈ Cut the red and green sweet peppers into small squares.

≈ Scrub and dice the carrots.

≈ Heat the oil in a medium-sized heavy-bottomed pan, then add the whole dried chilli peppers, breaking them into the pan, and the cumin seeds. As they begin to sizzle, add the turmeric and salt. Stir, then add all the vegetables, including the tomato. Mix and simmer for 2 minutes.

≈ Add the ginger, garlic and green chillies and stir to blend everything together thoroughly.

≈ Then, lower the heat, cover the pan tightly and steam cook the vegetables for 12–15 minutes.

≈ Add the chopped coriander and serve.

SPICY GREEN BEANS

SERVES 4

Marinate these beans early in the day, and you'll have a spicy dish by dinner. These make an easy addition to a picnic or garden party.

≈ Cook the green beans in boiling water until just tender, 3–4 minutes. Drain and plunge into cold water, then drain well again.

≈ In a glass dish, or other non-reactive dish, whisk together all the remaining ingredients. Add the beans and stir to coat thoroughly. Refrigerate at least 3 hours. Serve cold.

1 lb (450 g) fresh green beans, topped and tailed

2 tbsp vegetable oil

2 tbsp white-wine vinegar

1 tbsp fresh-squeezed lemon juice

1 tsp Creole mustard

1 garlic clove, finely chopped

1 spring onion, finely chopped

1 tsp red chilli pepper flakes

¼ tsp salt

NUTRITION FACTS	
Amount per Serving	
Calories 79	Calories from Fat 54
	% Daily Value
Total Fat 6g	9%
Saturated Fat 1g	15%
Polyunsaturated Fat 4g	0%
Monounsaturated Fat 1g	0%
Cholesterol 0mg	0%
Sodium 15mg	0.6%
Total Carbohydrate 4g	1%
Dietary Fibre 3.5g	14%
Sugars 3g	0%
Protein 2g	0%

Percent daily values are based on a 2000 calorie diet

PINEAPPLE AND CHILLI PEPPER RICE

SERVES 4

1 large or 2 medium fresh pineapples

2 tbsp sunflower oil

1 red sweet pepper, seeded and chopped

8 oz (225 g) courgettes, trimmed and diced

6 spring onions, trimmed and sliced diagonally

10 oz (285 g) cooked long-grain rice

6 jarred jalapeño chilli peppers, drained and chopped

salt and freshly ground black pepper

2 tbsp pine nuts, toasted

3 tbsp freshly chopped coriander

grated low-fat cheese

≈ Cut the pineapple in half lengthways through the plume and scoop out the flesh. Reserve the two halves. Discard the central core, dice the remaining flesh and reserve.

≈ Heat the oil in a pan and sauté the red pepper and courgettes for 5 minutes, or until softened. Add the spring onions and sauté for a further minute. Stir the rice with the chilli peppers, seasoning, and the reserved pineapple flesh.

≈ Heat gently, stirring occasionally, for 5 minutes, or until hot. Then stir in the pine nuts and coriander. Pile into the reserved pineapple shells and serve with grated low-fat cheese.

NUTRITION FACTS

Amount per Serving

Calories 267	Calories from Fat 80
	% Daily Value
Total Fat 9g	14%
Saturated Fat 1g	5%
Polyunsaturated Fat 5g	0%
Monounsaturated Fat 2g	0%
Cholesterol 2mg	0.6%
Sodium 9mg	0.4%
Total Carbohydrate 42g	14%
Dietary Fibre 4.5g	18%
Sugars 19g	0%
Protein 7g	0%

Percent daily values are based on a 2000 calorie diet

HERBED CAULIFLOWER

SERVES 4

*Cauliflower cheese traditionally has a rich cheese sauce coating the cauliflower.
This low-fat version uses a wine and herb sauce which is equally delicious.*

4 baby cauliflowers

2 mint sprigs

900 ml (1½ pints) vegetable stock

25 g (1 oz) low-fat cheese, grated

For the sauce

150 ml (¼ pint) vegetable stock

300 ml (½ pint) skimmed milk

150 ml (¼ pint) dry white wine

30 g (2 tbsp) cornflour

15 g (1 tbsp) fresh chopped parsley

15 g (1 tbsp) fresh chopped
coriander

15 g (1 tbsp) fresh chopped thyme

ground black pepper

NUTRITION FACTS	
Serving Size 1 (846g)	
Calories 160	Calories from Fat 27
	% Daily Value
Total Fat 3g	4%
Saturated Fat 0g	2%
Monounsaturated Fat 0.1g	0%
Polyunsaturated Fat 0.0g	0%
Cholesterol 4mg	1%
Sodium 1309mg	55%
Total Carbohydrate 24g	8%
Dietary Fibre 12g	46%
Sugars 18g	0%
Protein 16g	0%

Per cent daily values are based on a 2000 calorie diet

≈ Trim the cauliflowers and place in a large pan with the mint and stock. Cook gently for 10 minutes.

≈ Meanwhile, place the stock for the sauce, the milk and white wine in a pan. Blend the cornflour with 60 ml (4 tablespoons) of cold water and add to the pan. Bring to the boil, stirring, and add the herbs. Season and simmer for 2–3 minutes.

≈ Drain the cauliflower and place in an ovenproof dish. Pour on the sauce and top with the cheese. Grill for 2–3 minutes until the cheese has melted. Serve.

RATATOUILLE

SERVES 4

A medley of vegetables cooked in a tomato and herb sauce. This is a strongly flavoured dish to be served with a plainer recipe or used to top a jacket potato.

1 onion, halved and sliced

2 garlic cloves, crushed

150 ml (¼ pint) vegetable stock

1 large aubergine, sliced

175 g (6 oz) courgettes, sliced

1 green pepper, seeded and sliced

30 ml (2 tbsp) tomato purée

400 g (14 oz) can chopped tomatoes

30 g (2 tbsp) fresh chopped oregano

ground black pepper

NUTRITION FACTS	
Serving Size 1 (351g)	
Calories 83	Calories from Fat 9
	% Daily Value
Total Fat 1g	1%
Saturated Fat 0g	0%
Monounsaturated Fat 0.0g	0%
Polyunsaturated Fat 0.1g	0%
Cholesterol 0mg	0%
Sodium 228mg	10%
Total Carbohydrate 17g	6%
Dietary Fibre 3g	12%
Sugars 2g	0%
Protein 4g	0%

Per cent daily values are based on a 2000 calorie diet

≈ Place the onion, garlic, and stock in a frying pan and cook for 5 minutes until the onion softens. Add the aubergine, courgettes and yellow pepper and cook for a further 5 minutes.

≈ Stir in the tomato purée, chopped tomatoes and 15 g (1 tablespoon) of the oregano. Season well. Bring to the boil, cover and reduce the heat. Cook for 1 hour, stirring occasionally. Sprinkle with the remaining oregano and serve.

STUFFED PEPPERS

SERVES 4

These peppers are filled with bulgur wheat flavoured with cheese, vegetables and fruit. Serve as an accompaniment or as a meal in themselves.

115 g (4 oz) bulgur wheat

250 ml (8 fl oz) vegetable stock

4 red peppers

1.5 g (¼ tsp) ground turmeric

40 g (1½ oz) mushrooms, diced

30 g (2 tbsp) raisins

30 g (2 tbsp) dried apricots, diced

3 spring onions, sliced

25 g (1 oz) low-fat cheese, grated

30 g (2 tbsp) fresh chopped coriander

1.5 g (¼ tsp) cayenne pepper

ground black pepper

≈ Place the bulgur wheat in a bowl and pour on the vegetable stock. Stand for 30 minutes. Drain if required.

≈ Meanwhile, cut the tops from the peppers and remove the core and seeds. Cook the peppers in boiling water for 2 minutes, drain and refresh under cold water.

≈ Mix together the remaining ingredients. Stir into the bulgur wheat and spoon into the peppers. Season with black pepper.

≈ Stand the peppers in a shallow oven-proof dish and pour in enough boiling water to come halfway up the sides. Cover and cook in the oven at 180°C (350°F, Gas 4) for 20 minutes. Serve.

NUTRITION FACTS	
Serving Size 1 (268g)	
Calories 209	Calories from Fat 9
	% Daily Value
Total Fat 1g	2%
Saturated Fat 0g	1%
Monounsaturated Fat 0.1g	0%
Polyunsaturated Fat 0.2g	0%
Cholesterol 2mg	1%
Sodium 274mg	11%
Total Carbohydrate 44g	15%
Dietary Fibre 8g	32%
Sugars 3g	0%
Protein 8g	0%

Per cent daily values are based on a 2000 calorie diet

MINTED BEANS AND CUCUMBER

SERVES 4

Cucumber is not usually served hot, but it is cooked perfectly with the beans in this recipe and delicately flavoured with mint. An unusual but delicious side dish.

450 g (1 lb) French beans, trimmed

½ cucumber, thickly sliced

2 garlic cloves, crushed

4 mint sprigs

15 ml (1 tbsp) lemon juice

75 ml (3 fl oz) vegetable stock

ground black pepper

strips of lemon zest for garnish

≈ Prepare the vegetables and place on a large sheet of foil. Bring up the sides of the foil around the vegetables and crimp to form an open parcel. Add the remaining ingredients, season and seal the top of the parcel.

≈ Place the parcel in a steamer and cook for 25 minutes or until the beans are tender. Garnish and serve.

NUTRITION FACTS	
Serving Size 1 (185g)	
Calories 40	Calories from Fat 9
	% Daily Value
Total Fat 1g	2%
Saturated Fat 0g	1%
Monounsaturated Fat 0.4g	0%
Polyunsaturated Fat 0.3g	0%
Cholesterol 0mg	0%
Sodium 106mg	4%
Total Carbohydrate 6g	2%
Dietary Fibre 2g	9%
Sugars 3g	0%
Protein 2g	0%

Per cent daily values are based on a 2000 calorie diet

Minted Beans and Cucumber ▶

SPICED AUBERGINES

SERVES 4

An Indian aubergine dish which is perfect with curry or a plain vegetable casserole. Spicy in itself, it is also delicious cold as an appetizer.

450 g (1 lb) aubergines

175 g (6 oz) potatoes

60 ml (4 tbsp) vegetable stock

½ onion, sliced

1 small red pepper, seeded and diced

1.5 g (¼ tsp) ground coriander

1.5 g (¼ tsp) ground cumin

5 g (1 tsp) root ginger, grated

2.5 g (½ tsp) curry powder

3 garlic cloves, crushed

5 g (1 tsp) chilli powder

dash of ground turmeric

dash of sugar

1 green chilli, diced

15 g (1 tbsp) fresh chopped coriander

NUTRITION FACTS	
Serving Size 1 (206g)	
Calories 110	Calories from Fat 9
	% Daily Value
Total Fat 1g	1%
Saturated Fat 0g	0%
Monounsaturated Fat 0.0g	0%
Polyunsaturated Fat 0.1g	0%
Cholesterol 0mg	0%
Sodium 78mg	3%
Total Carbohydrate 25g	8%
Dietary Fibre 5g	20%
Sugars 3g	0%
Protein 3g	0%

Per cent daily values are based on a 2000 calorie diet

≈ Dice the aubergines into small cubes. Cut the potatoes into 2.5 cm (1 in) chunks.

≈ Heat the stock in a pan, add the onion and cook for 2–3 minutes. Stir in the red pepper, ground coriander, cumin, ginger, curry powder, garlic, chilli powder and turmeric, and cook for 2–3 minutes.

≈ Add the aubergine, sugar, green chilli and 150 ml (¼ pint) water, cover and simmer for 15 minutes. Add the potato, re-cover and cook for 10 minutes. Stir in the fresh coriander and serve.

STEAMED HONEY-GLAZED PARSNIPS

SERVES 4

Traditionally parsnips are roasted or baked, but they steam equally well and in far less time.

≈ Cook the parsnips in boiling water for 5 minutes. Drain well and place in a steamer lined with foil.

≈ Mix together the honey, ginger, cumin seeds, vegetable stock and coriander. Pour over the parsnips and season.

. Cover and steam for 20 minutes or until cooked through. Serve immediately with the cooking liquid.

8 baby parsnips

30 ml (2 tbsp) honey

2.5 g (½ tsp) ground ginger

2.5 g (½ tsp) cumin seeds

125 ml (4 fl oz) vegetable stock

15 g (1 tbsp) fresh chopped coriander

ground black pepper

NUTRITION FACTS	
Serving Size 1 (100g)	
Calories 90	Calories from Fat 0
	% Daily Value
Total Fat 0g	1%
Saturated Fat 0g	0%
Monounsaturated Fat 0.1g	0%
Polyunsaturated Fat 0.0g	0%
Cholesterol 0mg	0%
Sodium 80mg	3%
Total Carbohydrate 22g	7%
Dietary Fibre 3g	13%
Sugars 9g	0%
Protein 2g	0%

Per cent daily values are based on a 2000 calorie diet

MIXED VEGETABLE DUMPLINGS

MAKES 24

These are like Chinese dumplings or Dim Sum. A water and flour dough encases delicately chopped vegetables. Quickly steamed they are perfect with a Chinese main course.

≈ Mix all the filling ingredients together in a bowl.

≈ Place 275 g (10 oz) of the flour for the dough in a bowl. Stir in 125 ml (4 fl oz) boiling water, 60 ml (4 tablespoons) cold water and the oil. Bring the mixture together to form a dough. Sprinkle the remaining flour on a work surface and knead the dough until smooth. Roll the dough into a long sausage shape and cut into 24 equal pieces. Roll each piece into a 5 cm (2 in) round.

≈ Divide the filling into 24 and spoon into the centre of each round. Bring the edges of the dough together in the centre and pinch together to seal as a parcel.

≈ Line a steamer with a damp cloth, place one-quarter of the dumplings in the steamer and steam for 5 minutes. Repeat with the remaining dumplings and serve.

For the filling

1 small carrot, finely chopped

1 celery stick, chopped

1 spring onion, chopped

1 small courgette, finely chopped

2 garlic cloves, crushed

7.5 ml (½ tbsp) soya sauce

dash of sugar

5 ml (1 tsp) dry sherry

15 g (1 tbsp) cornflour

For the dough

350 g (12 oz) plain flour

15 ml (1 tbsp) polyunsaturated oil

NUTRITION FACTS	
Serving Size 1 (29g)	
Calories 68	Calories from Fat 9
	% Daily Value
Total Fat 1g	1%
Saturated Fat 0g	0%
Monounsaturated Fat 0.0g	0%
Polyunsaturated Fat 0.4g	0%
Cholesterol 0mg	0%
Sodium 25mg	1%
Total Carbohydrate 13g	4%
Dietary Fibre 1g	3%
Sugars 1g	0%
Protein 2g	0%

Per cent daily values are based on a 2000 calorie diet

175 g (6 oz) red lentils

20 ml (4 tsp) polyunsaturated oil

1 red onion, chopped

2 garlic cloves, crushed

1.5 g (¼ tsp) ground cumin

1.5 g (¼ tsp) ground coriander

1 red chilli, chopped

900 ml (1½ pints) vegetable stock

juice and grated zest of 1 lime

ground black pepper

NUTRITION FACTS

Serving Size 1 (237g)

Calories 186	Calories from Fat 45
	% Daily Value
Total Fat 5g	8%
Saturated Fat 0g	2%
Monounsaturated Fat 0.6g	0%
Polyunsaturated Fat 3.5g	0%
Cholesterol 0mg	0%
Sodium 59mg	2%
Total Carbohydrate 23g	8%
Dietary Fibre 12g	46%
Sugars 0g	0%
Protein 14g	0%

Per cent daily values are based on a 2000 calorie diet

40 g (1½ oz) open cap mushrooms

75 g (3 oz) oyster mushrooms

50 g (2 oz) shiitake mushrooms

60 ml (4 tbsp) vegetable stock

2 garlic cloves, crushed

15 ml (1 tbsp) soya sauce

30 g (2 tbsp) fresh chopped parsley
    or thyme

ground black pepper

NUTRITION FACTS

Serving Size 1 (129g)

Calories 71	Calories from Fat 0
	% Daily Value
Total Fat 0g	1%
Saturated Fat 0g	1%
Monounsaturated Fat 0.1g	0%
Polyunsaturated Fat 0.0g	0%
Cholesterol 0mg	0%
Sodium 289mg	12%
Total Carbohydrate 18g	6%
Dietary Fibre 3g	12%
Sugars 0g	0%
Protein 2g	0%

Per cent daily values are based on a 2000 calorie diet

HOT SPICY LENTILS

SERVES 4

An example of using lentils in place of meat, this recipe can be eaten as a side dish or as a vegetarian meal.

≈ Wash the lentils in 2–3 changes of water. Drain and reserve. Heat the oil in a pan, add the onion, garlic, and spices and cook for 5 minutes. Stir in the lentils and cook for a further 3–4 minutes.

≈ Add the chilli and stock and bring to the boil. Reduce the heat and simmer gently for 35 minutes until the lentils are soft. Stir in the lime juice and rind. Season well and serve.

THREE-MUSHROOM FRY

SERVES 4

This really is a simple yet delicious dish. Three varieties of mushroom are cooked in garlic and soya sauce.

≈ Peel the open cap mushrooms and thinly slice. Place all the mushrooms in a frying pan with the stock, garlic, soya sauce and half of the herbs. Season well with black pepper. Cook, stirring, for 3–4 minutes. Sprinkle in the remaining herbs and serve immediately.

Three-Mushroom Fry ▶

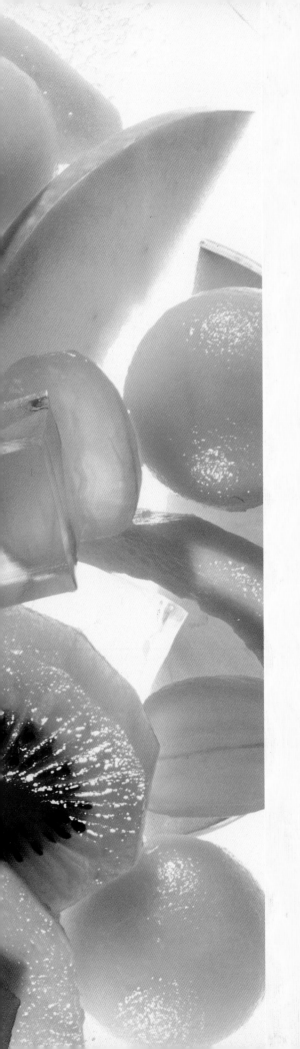

DESSERTS

APRICOT RING

SERVES 6

With its golden colour and glistening texture, this is a very appealing dessert, and one that has the hidden benefit of a high fibre content provided by the apricots.

3 oz (85 g) light brown unrefined
    sugar
1 small orange
1 pt (½ l) water
1 lb (450 g) cooking apples, peeled,
    cored and sliced
¾ lb (340 g) dried apricot pieces,
    soaked overnight and drained
2 tbsp powdered gelatine

Decoration
herb leaves

≈ Put the sugar, a strip of the orange rind, and the water in a pan and bring it slowly to a boil, stirring occasionally to dissolve the sugar. Fast-boil for 3 minutes, and then add the apple slices and poach them over low heat for about 8 minutes, or until they become translucent and are just tender. Lift out the apple slices with a slotted spoon and set them aside.

≈ Add the apricots and the juice of the orange to the syrup, bring to a boil, and simmer for 20 minutes or until the fruit is tender. Discard the orange rind, and purée the fruit thoroughly in a blender or food processor.

≈ Sprinkle the gelatin on to 3 tablespoons of hot water in a small bowl. Stand the bowl in a pan of hot water, and stir to dissolve the crystals. Stir the solution into the apricot purée and set aside to cool.

≈ Rinse a 2-pint (1-litre) ring mould with cold water. Arrange the apple slices in the base, and spoon on the apricot purée. Cover the mould and chill it in the refrigerator for about 2 hours, or until it has set firmly.

≈ Run a knife around the sides of the mould, and dip it quickly in and out of hot water. Place a flat serving plate over the mould, invert it quickly, and shake to release the fruit. Decorate the ring with herb leaves.

BLACKCURRANT SORBET

SERVES 4

It is reassuring to have a fruit sorbet stored in the freezer, a luxurious standby for unexpected visitors for dinner or an extra-busy occasion.

≈ Put the blackcurrants, honey, sugar and water into a saucepan, and bring slowly to a boil, stirring occasionally. Simmer for 15 minutes, or until the fruit is soft. Allow to cool.

≈ Rub the fruit and juice through a sieve, and place it in a metal ice-cube tray or a plastic freezer box. Cover with foil or a lid, and freeze for 1–2 hours, until the mixture is mushy and starting to set on the outside.

≈ Beat the egg whites until stiff. Turn the fruit purée out into a chilled bowl and fold in the egg whites.

≈ Return the mixture to the container, cover, and freeze for another 2 hours, or until firm. Stir it once or twice.

≈ To serve, allow the sorbet to soften a little in the refrigerator for about 30 minutes. Spoon or scoop it into four individual serving glasses, and top each one with a mint sprig if you wish.

1 lb (450 g) blackcurrants, fresh or frozen

4 tbsp clear honey

3½ oz (100 g) sugar

5 fl oz (150 ml) water

2 egg whites

Decoration

mint sprigs (optional)

NUTRITION FACTS	
Amount per Serving	
Calories 189	Calories from Fat 0
	% Daily Value
Total Fat 0g	0%
Saturated Fat 0g	0%
Polyunsaturated Fat 0g	0%
Monounsaturated Fat 0g	0%
Cholesterol 0mg	0%
Sodium 37mg	1.5%
Total Carbohydrate 48g	16%
Dietary Fibre 5.5g	22%
Sugars 48g	0%
Protein 2.5g	0%

Percent daily values are based on a 2000 calorie diet

BAKED RHUBARB WITH OAT TOPPING

SERVES 4

Family members who like old-fashioned puddings will love this sticky-toffee fruit layer topped with a healthful and delicious crunchy oat mixture.

1 lb (450 g) rhubarb, trimmed and cut into 1-in (2.5-cm) lengths

grated rind and juice of 1 orange

1 tbsp water

2 oz (60 g) pitted dates, chopped

2 tbsp clear honey

Topping

7½ oz (210 g) wholemeal breadcrumbs

5 oz (140 g) rolled oats

3 oz (85 g) polyunsaturated margarine, melted

2 oz (60 g) light brown unrefined sugar

≈ Set the oven to 180°C/350°F/Gas 4. Place the rhubarb, orange juice and rind, water, dates and honey in a 2½ pint (1.5 litre) ovenproof dish.

≈ For the topping, mix together the breadcrumbs, oats, margarine and sugar, and spread the topping over the fruit. Bake in the oven for about 35 minutes, until the topping is golden. Serve piping hot.

NUTRITION FACTS	
Amount per Serving	
Calories 379	Calories from Fat 162
	% Daily Value
Total Fat 18g	28%
Saturated Fat 4g	20%
Polyunsaturated Fat 8g	0%
Monounsaturated Fat 6g	0%
Cholesterol 0mg	0%
Sodium 262mg	11%
Total Carbohydrate 51g	17%
Dietary Fibre 7g	28%
Sugars 28g	0%
Protein 6g	0%

Percent daily values are based on a 2000 calorie diet

SLICED EXOTIC FRUITS WITH DATES

SERVES 6

Fruit salad has always been a popular dessert and almost any seasonal fruits are delicious sliced or cut up together in their natural juices or with a fruit purée. This is not a traditional fruit salad, but a selection of exotic fruits, sliced and served together. Ogen melons from Israel are as sweet as sugar, as are the Israeli oranges. California produces a wonderful variety of date, the Medjool date, which is recommended for this dish.

1 ogen or canteloupe melon, seeded and sliced in thin wedges and peeled

3 sweet seedless oranges, peeled and segmented, juice reserved

1 mango, peeled and thinly sliced

24 fresh lychees, peeled, or 1 16-oz (450 g) tin lychees in their own juice

12 Medjool dates, cut in half lengthwise and pitted

1 pomegranate, cut in half, seeds reserved (optional)

Garnish
fresh mint leaves

≈ Arrange slices of melon on each of six individual plates in a fan shape. Arrange peeled orange segments and mango slices in an attractive pattern over the melon slices.

≈ Evenly distribute fresh or tinned lychees over fruit and sprinkle on some reserved juices from all fruits.

≈ Arrange four date halves on each plate and sprinkle with the pomegranate seeds, if using. Garnish with fresh mint leaves and serve.

NUTRITION FACTS	
Amount per Serving	
Calories 165	Calories from Fat 4
	% Daily Value
Total Fat 0.4g	0.6%
Saturated Fat 0.03g	0.15%
Polyunsaturated Fat 0.03g	0%
Monounsaturated Fat 0.03g	0%
Cholesterol 0mg	0%
Sodium 31mg	1%
Total Carbohydrate 40g	13%
Dietary Fibre 6.5g	26%
Sugars 38g	0%
Protein 3g	0%

Percent daily values are based on a 2000 calorie diet

ORANGE SORBET

SERVES 6

Citrus fruit sorbets and ices make an ideal dessert choice after any meal. Adding beaten egg whites gives sorbet a very smooth, creamy texture. If you prefer a rougher, "icier" texture, omit the whites. Processing the mixture breaks up the ice crystals and contributes to a smooth texture.

8 fl oz (250 ml) water

8 oz (225 g) sugar

grated zest and juice of 1 lemon

grated zest of 3 oranges

1 pt (½ l) fresh-squeezed orange
     juice, strained

2 egg whites, beaten to soft peaks

fresh mint leaves for garnish

Cointreau for serving

≈ In a small heavy saucepan, combine sugar, lemon and orange zests and the water. Slowly bring to a boil, stirring until sugar dissolves. Cook 5 minutes; remove from heat and cool and refrigerate 3–4 hours or overnight.

≈ Combine lemon and orange juices with the chilled syrup and, if you like, strain for a very smooth sorbet.

≈ If using an ice-cream machine, freeze according to manufacturer's directions.

≈ Alternatively, put into a metal bowl and freeze 3–4 hours until semifrozen. Into a food processor fitted with metal blade. Scrape the semifrozen mixture; process until light and creamy, 30–45 seconds. Return to the metal bowl and freeze another 1½ hours. Scrape into food processor again and process with beaten egg whites until well mixed and light and creamy, 30 seconds. Freeze 3–4 hours until completely firm.

≈ Soften 5 minutes at room temperature before scooping into individual serving glasses. Garnish with a few mint leaves and pass the liqueur, allowing each guest to pour a little over sorbet.

NUTRITION FACTS	
Amount per Serving	
Calories 178	Calories from Fat 0
	% Daily Value
Total Fat 0g	0%
Saturated Fat 0g	0%
Polyunsaturated Fat 0g	0%
Monounsaturated Fat 0g	0%
Cholesterol 0mg	0%
Sodium 24mg	1%
Total Carbohydrate 46g	15%
Dietary Fibre 1g	4%
Sugars 46g	0%
Protein 1g	0%

Percent daily values are based on a 2000 calorie diet

APRICOT PRALINE PAVLOVA

SERVES 6

A spectacular dessert to draw delighted comments at the end of a special meal, and proof that pavlova, a filled meringue basket, does not have to be filled with whipped cream.

½ lb (225 g) dried apricot pieces

10 oz (300 ml) orange juice

6 oz (180 g) plain low-fat yogurt

Praline

6 tbsp set honey

1 oz caster sugar

4 oz (115 g) chopped blanched
    almonds

oil, for brushing

Meringue

3 egg whites

5 oz (150 g) granulated sugar

≈ Soak the apricots in the orange juice for at least 2 hours, or overnight; place in a pan, bring to a boil, and simmer for 20 minutes until the fruit is tender. Allow to cool, then purée the apricots and any remaining juice in a blender or food processor and beat in the yogurt.

≈ To make the praline, put the honey and 2 tablespoons sugar into a small pan and bring to a boil. Boil for 5 minutes, until very thick. Remove from the heat, and stir in the almonds. Pour into an oiled tin, and leave to cool.

≈ Set the oven to 135°C/275°F/Gas 1. To make the meringue, whisk the egg whites until they are very stiff. Fold in half the sugar, and whisk again until the mixture is stiff and glossy. Fold in the remaining sugar.

≈ Line a baking tray with waxed paper, and spoon the meringue to make a nest. Bake in the oven for 1 hour, or until the meringue is firm. Leave it to cool, then peel off the paper, and place it on a serving dish.

≈ Coarsely crush the praline with a rolling pin or in the blender. Just before serving, spoon the apricot mixture into the centre of the meringue, and sprinkle on the praline.

NUTRITION FACTS	
Amount per Serving	
Calories 366	Calories from Fat 90
	% Daily Value
Total Fat 10g	15%
Saturated Fat 1g	5%
Polyunsaturated Fat 3g	0%
Monounsaturated Fat 6g	0%
Cholesterol 1mg	0.3%
Sodium 79mg	3%
Total Carbohydrate 64g	21%
Dietary Fibre 6g	24%
Sugars 64g	0%
Protein 8g	0%

Percent daily values are based on a 2000 calorie diet

PINEAPPLE MERINGUE

SERVES 6

Pineapple rings, grilled until they are toasty-brown and then topped with fluffy meringue, make an impressive dessert for a dinner party.

≈ Line the grilling tray with foil. In a small bowl mix together the raisins, orange juice and orange rind, and set aside for a few minutes.

≈ Brush the pineapple rings with half the margarine, and grill them for 4–5 minutes (at medium heat), until they are brown. Turn the rings, brush the other side with the remaining margarine, and grill for another 4–5 minutes.

≈ Whisk the egg whites until they are stiff. Whisk in half the sugar, and continue beating until the mixture is stiff and glossy. Fold in the remaining sugar and the nuts.

≈ Spoon the raisin mixture into the centre of the pineapple rings, and cover them with the meringue. Grill for 2–3 minutes, until the topping is streaked with brown. Serve hot.

2 oz (60 g) sultanas

2 tbsp orange juice

1 tsp grated orange rind

1 pineapple, peeled, cored and sliced into 6 rings

2 tbsp polyunsaturated margarine, melted

Meringue

2 egg whites

4½ oz (130 g) light brown sugar

2 tbsp chopped almonds, toasted

NUTRITION FACTS	
Amount per Serving	
Calories 162	Calories from Fat 54
	% Daily Value
Total Fat 6g	9%
Saturated Fat 1g	5%
Polyunsaturated Fat 2g	0%
Monounsaturated Fat 3g	0%
Cholesterol 0mg	0%
Sodium 62mg	2.5%
Total Carbohydrate 26g	9%
Dietary Fibre 1.5g	6%
Sugars 26g	0%
Protein 2g	0%

Percent daily values are based on a 2000 calorie diet

SUMMER PUDDING

SERVES 6

This traditional English pudding is a delightful way to celebrate the berry harvest or to use a store of frozen berries.

2¼ lb (1 kg) mixed berries such as raspberries, gooseberries and blackcurrants

4 tbsp light or brown unrefined sugar, or to taste

3–4 tbsp water

about 8 slices wholemeal bread cut from a large loaf, crusts removed

Garnish

scented herb leaves (optional)

NUTRITION FACTS	
Amount per Serving	
Calories 189	Calories from Fat 18
	% Daily Value
Total Fat 2g	3%
Saturated Fat 0.3g	1.5%
Polyunsaturated Fat 0.4g	0%
Monounsaturated Fat 0.3g	0%
Cholesterol 0mg	0%
Sodium 302mg	12.5%
Total Carbohydrate 39g	13%
Dietary Fibre 11g	44%
Sugars 17g	0%
Protein 7g	0%

Percent daily values are based on a 2000 calorie diet

≈ Prepare the fruit as required: hull raspberries, top and tail gooseberries, and strip blackcurrants from the stalks. Put the fruit into a large pan with the sugar and water, and cook over a low heat until the sugar dissolves and the juices start to run. Cook gently until all the fruit is just tender – about 15 minutes.

≈ Cut the bread slices to line a 2-pint bowl. Fit the bread around the container so that there are no gaps.

≈ Tip the fruit into the bowl and cover the top with more bread slices so that the fruit is completely enclosed. Place a saucer or small plate over the container and press it down with a heavy weight.

≈ Leave the pudding in the refrigerator for several hours or overnight. To unmould the pudding, run a knife blade between the bowl and the bread lining, place a serving plate over the top, invert both pudding and plate, and shake sharply to release the pudding. Decorate with the herb leaves.

DAIRY MOULDS

SERVES 6

A delicious low-fat version of the French coeur à la crème, *this dairy blend makes a light and delightful accompaniment to berries of all kinds.*

1 lb (450 g) low-fat cottage cheese

6 oz (180 g) plain low-fat yogurt

3 tbsp warm water

1 tbsp powdered gelatine

≈ Strain the cottage cheese into a bowl. Beat in the yogurt.

≈ Pour the water into a small bowl, sprinkle on the gelatin, stir well, and stand the bowl in a pan of warm water. Leave for about 5 minutes for the gelatine to dissolve. Pour the gelatine mixture into the cheese and beat well.

≈ Spoon the cheese into 6 individual moulds. Heart-shaped ones are traditional, or you can improvise by using ramekin dishes or yogurt tubs covered with cheesecloth and inverted. Stand the moulds on a wire rack over a plate and leave them to drain in the refrigerator overnight.

≈ Turn out the moulds, and serve well chilled.

NUTRITION FACTS	
Amount per Serving	
Calories 88	Calories from Fat 9
	% Daily Value
Total Fat 1g	1.5%
Saturated Fat 1g	5%
Polyunsaturated Fat 0g	0%
Monounsaturated Fat 0g	0%
Cholesterol 5mg	1.6%
Sodium 324mg	13.5%
Total Carbohydrate 5g	1.6%
Dietary Fibre 0g	0%
Sugars 5g	0%
Protein 14.5g	0%

Percent daily values are based on a 2000 calorie diet

MIXED FRUIT COMPOTE

SERVES 10

The perfect accompaniment to this delicious dessert is low-fat yogurt.

12 oz (340 g) pears

12 oz (340 g) apples

12 oz (340 g) peaches

12 oz (340 g) apricots

2 tbsp freshly squeezed lemon juice

1½ lb (675 g) caster sugar

2 cinnamon sticks

2 pts (1 l) water

3–4 whole cloves

strip of lemon peel

NUTRITION FACTS	
Amount per Serving	
Calories 268	Calories from Fat 1
	% Daily Value
Total Fat 0.1g	0.2%
Saturated Fat 0g	0%
Polyunsaturated Fat 0g	0%
Monounsaturated Fat 0g	0%
Cholesterol 0mg	0%
Sodium 6mg	0.25%
Total Carbohydrate 70g	2.3%
Dietary Fibre 2g	8%
Sugars 70g	0%
Protein 1g	0%

Percent daily values are based on a 2000 calorie diet

≈ To prepare the fruit for the compote, peel, core, and quarter the pears and apples. Wash the peaches and apricots, and remove the pits. Cut the peaches into quarters and the apricots in half.
≈ Place the pear and apple quarters in a large, heavy-based saucepan with the lemon juice, sugar, cinnamon sticks, water, cloves and lemon peel. Gently bring to a boil and simmer for 5 minutes.

≈ Add the peaches and cook for a further 5 minutes, then add the apricot halves and continue to cook for 3–5 minutes or until softened. Using a slotted spoon, transfer the fruit to a serving bowl, cover and set aside.
≈ Return the syrup to a boil and continue to boil rapidly for about 10 minutes, or until reduced slightly and thickened. Remove the cinnamon sticks, cloves, and lemon peel. Allow the syrup to cool, then pour over the fruit. Serve at room temperature or chilled.

MELON AND WALNUT COMPOTE

SERVES 6

Versions of this simple dessert are eaten from Greece through Georgia and Armenia to Uzbekistan.

2 small cantaloupe or honeydew melons, halved, seeded and cubed

12 fl oz (340 ml) honey

1 lb (450 g) walnuts, chopped

NUTRITION FACTS	
Amount per Serving	
Calories 267	Calories from Fat 95
	% Daily Value
Total Fat 10.5g	16%
Saturated Fat 1g	5%
Polyunsaturated Fat 7g	0%
Monounsaturated Fat 2g	0%
Cholesterol 0mg	0%
Sodium 69mg	3%
Total Carbohydrate 42g	14%
Dietary Fibre 2.5g	10%
Sugars 42g	0%
Protein 3.5g	0%

Percent daily values are based on a 2000 calorie diet

≈ Place the melon cubes, with any juice, in a bowl. Add the honey and toss to coat lightly. Stir in the walnuts. Divide the mixture among individual bowls.

HONEYED ORANGES

SERVES 4

Oranges and ginger make a great combination. Ground ginger has been added to this recipe with a dash of orange liqueur for extra flavour.

60 ml (4 tbsp) honey

2.5 g (½ tsp) ground cinnamon

1.5 g (¼ tsp) ground ginger

2 mint sprigs

10 ml (2 tsp) Grand Marnier

4 oranges

≈ Place the honey, cinnamon, ginger and mint in a pan with 150 ml (¼ pint) water. Heat gently to melt the honey. Bring to the boil and boil for 3 minutes to reduce by half. Remove the mint from the pan and discard. Stir in the Grand Marnier.

≈ Meanwhile, peel the oranges, remove the pith and slice thinly. Place the orange slices in a serving bowl, pour over the syrup and chill for 1 hour before serving.

NUTRITION FACTS	
Serving Size 1 (253g)	
Calories 141	Calories from Fat 0
	% Daily Value
Total Fat 0g	1%
Saturated Fat 0g	0%
Monounsaturated Fat 0.0g	0%
Polyunsaturated Fat 0.0g	0%
Cholesterol 0mg	0%
Sodium 4mg	0%
Total Carbohydrate 34g	11%
Dietary Fibre 10g	40%
Sugars 37g	0%
Protein 2g	0%

Per cent daily values are based on a 2000 calorie diet

STRAWBERRY FOOL

SERVES 4

This dish is simple to prepare, but should be made in advance of a meal as it requires chilling for 1 hour before serving.

275 g (10 oz) strawberries, hulled and chopped

50 g (2 oz) icing sugar

300 ml (½ pint) low-fat natural yogurt

2 egg whites

strawberry slices and mint sprigs to decorate

≈ Place the chopped strawberries in a food processor with the icing sugar. Liquidize for 30 seconds until smooth.

≈ Place the yogurt in a bowl and stir in the strawberry mixture. Whisk the egg whites until peaks form and fold in gently. Spoon into serving glasses and chill for 1 hour. Decorate and serve.

NUTRITION FACTS	
Serving Size 1 (181g)	
Calories 136	Calories from Fat 9
	% Daily Value
Total Fat 1g	2%
Saturated Fat 1g	4%
Monounsaturated Fat 0.3g	0%
Polyunsaturated Fat 0.1g	0%
Cholesterol 4mg	1%
Sodium 79mg	3%
Total Carbohydrate 25g	8%
Dietary Fibre 2g	7%
Sugars 8g	0%
Protein 6g	0%

Per cent daily values are based on a 2000 calorie diet

Honeyed Oranges ▶

FRUDITÉES

SERVES 4

A sweet variation of "cruditées", this recipe is simple and easy to eat. An informal dessert to be shared with friends.

150 g (5 oz) strawberries, halved

1 green eating apple, cored and sliced

2 bananas, cut into 2.5 cm (1 in) chunks

1 kiwi fruit, cut into eight

10 ml (2 tsp) lemon juice

fresh mint to decorate

For the yogurt dip

250 ml (8 fl oz) low-fat natural yogurt

15 g (1 tbsp) soft brown sugar

dash of ground cinnamon

1 small papaya, seeded and diced

mint and cinnamon to decorate

NUTRITION FACTS	
Serving Size 1 (268g)	
Calories 162	Calories from Fat 18
	% Daily Value
Total Fat 2g	3%
Saturated Fat 1g	4%
Monounsaturated Fat 0.3g	0%
Polyunsaturated Fat 0.3g	0%
Cholesterol 3mg	1%
Sodium 44mg	2%
Total Carbohydrate 35g	12%
Dietary Fibre 5g	21%
Sugars 25g	0%
Protein 4g	0%

Per cent daily values are based on a 2000 calorie diet

≈ Prepare all the fruits. Sprinkle the apple and banana with the lemon juice.

≈ Place the yogurt dip ingredients in a food processor and liquidize for 30 seconds until smooth. Spoon into a serving bowl. Place the dip on a large serving plate, sprinkle with cinnamon, and arrange the fruit around. Serve with sprigs of mint.

BLUEBERRY CRUSH

SERVES 4

This is really quick to prepare, but requires freezing. Perfect to serve at a dinner party if you make it in advance.

≈ Place the meringues in a bowl. Add the blueberries and yogurt and mix well. Line a 750 ml (1¼ pint) pudding bowl with clingfilm and spoon in the mixture, pressing down well. Place in the freezer for 2 hours or until firm.

≈ Meanwhile for the sauce, place the blueberries, sugar and cranberry juice in a food processor. Liquidize for 30 seconds until smooth. Press through a sieve and chill until required.

≈ Dip the pudding bowl into hot water for 4 seconds. Invert the bowl onto a serving plate and unmould the pudding. Serve with the blueberry sauce.

150 g (5 oz) cooked meringue, broken into pieces
115 g (4 oz) blueberries
300 ml (1/2 pint) low-fat natural yogurt

For the sauce
115 g (4 oz) blueberries
30 g (2 tbsp) icing sugar
60 ml (4 tbsp) cranberry juice

NUTRITION FACTS	
Serving Size 1 (198g)	
Calories 216	Calories from Fat 9
	% Daily Value
Total Fat 1g	2%
Saturated Fat 1g	4%
Monounsaturated Fat 0.3g	0%
Polyunsaturated Fat 0.0g	0%
Cholesterol 4mg	1%
Sodium 97mg	4%
Total Carbohydrate 45g	15%
Dietary Fibre 2g	8%
Sugars 11g	0%
Protein 7g	0%

Per cent daily values are based on a 2000 calorie diet

APPLE CRUMBLE PIE

SERVES 8–12

A deep dish apple pie using filo or strudel pastry as the crust. Topped with a crumble mixture it is delicious served with natural yogurt.

≈ Lay a sheet of filo pastry in the base of a pie dish and up the sides. Brush lightly with melted margarine and continue layering pastry to cover the sides of the pie dish. Brush each sheet with margarine. Cook the pastry in the oven at 200°C (400°F, Gas 6) for 10 minutes.

≈ Meanwhile, place the apples, sugar, raisins and nutmeg in a pan. Cover and cook for 10 minutes or until the apples have softened. Mix together the topping ingredients.

≈ Spoon the apple filling into the pastry lined dish. Sprinkle on the topping, return to the oven and cook for 40 minutes until golden.

150 g (5 oz) filo pastry
25 g (1½ tbsp) polyunsaturated margarine, melted
900 g (2 lb) cooking apples, peeled and sliced
30 g (2 tbsp) soft brown sugar
30 g (2 tbsp) raisins
dash of grated nutmeg

For the topping
90 g (6 tbsp) plain flour
50 g (2 oz) porridge oats
50 g (2 oz) soft brown sugar
30 g (2 tbsp) polyunsaturated margarine

NUTRITION FACTS	
Serving Size 1 (161g)	
Calories 247	Calories from Fat 63
	% Daily Value
Total Fat 7g	11%
Saturated Fat 1g	6%
Monounsaturated Fat 2.5g	0%
Polyunsaturated Fat 2.3g	0%
Cholesterol 0mg	0%
Sodium 149mg	6%
Total Carbohydrate 45g	15%
Dietary Fibre 4g	16%
Sugars 11g	0%
Protein 3g	0%

Per cent daily values are based on a 2000 calorie diet

225 g (½ lb) bananas, chopped and
    frozen
15 ml (1 tbsp) lemon juice
90 g (6 tbsp) icing sugar
150 ml (¼ pint) low-fat natural yogurt
grated rind of 1 lemon
small meringues to serve (optional)

NUTRITION FACTS

Serving Size 1 (115g)

Calories 114	Calories from Fat 9
	% Daily Value
Total Fat 1g	1%
Saturated Fat 0g	2%
Monounsaturated Fat 0.2g	0%
Polyunsaturated Fat 0.0g	0%
Cholesterol 2mg	1%
Sodium 27mg	1%
Total Carbohydrate 32g	11%
Dietary Fibre 1g	6%
Sugars 20g	0%
Protein 3g	0%

Per cent daily values are based on a 2000 calorie diet

For the mousse
300 ml (½ pint) low-fat natural yogurt
150 ml (¼ pint) skimmed milk
    cheese or low-fat cream cheese
5 ml (1 tsp) vanilla extract
60 g (4 tbsp) vanilla sugar
15 ml (1 tbsp) brandy or sherry
15 g (1 tsp) vegetarian gelatine
2 large egg whites

For the sauce
300 g (1¾ cups) raspberries
juice of 1 orange
25 g (1 oz) icing sugar, sieved

NUTRITION FACTS

Serving Size 1 (248g)

Calories 373	Calories from Fat 9
	% Daily Value
Total Fat 1g	2%
Saturated Fat 1g	4%
Monounsaturated Fat 0.3g	0%
Polyunsaturated Fat 0.2g	0%
Cholesterol 4mg	1%
Sodium 82mg	3%
Total Carbohydrate 51g	17%
Dietary Fibre 3g	11%
Sugars 22g	0%
Protein 10g	0%

Per cent daily values are based on a 2000 calorie diet

BANANA ICE CREAM

SERVES 4

*This is really a cheat ice cream. Made with frozen bananas and natural yogurt,
the freezing time of the completed recipe is greatly reduced.*

≈ Set the freezer to rapid freeze. Place
the frozen bananas in a food processor
with the lemon juice, icing sugar and
yogurt. Process for 1 minute or until
smooth. Stir in the lemon rind.

≈ Place the mixture in a freezerproof
container, cover and freeze for 2 hours or
until set. Scoop into dishes and serve
with small meringues.

VANILLA MOUSSE

SERVES 4

*This light and fluffy mousse tastes as good as it looks. Sliced and served with the
raspberry sauce it is a dieter's dream.*

≈ Place the yogurt, cheese, vanilla
extract, sugar and alcohol in a food
processor, liquidize for 30 seconds until
smooth. Pour into a mixing bowl.
≈ Sprinkle the gelatine on to 60 ml
(4 tablespoons) of cold water. Stir until
dissolved and heat to boiling point. Boil
for 2 minutes. Cool. Stir into the
yogurt mixture. Whisk the egg whites
until peaking and fold into the mousse.

≈ Line a 900 ml (1½ pint) loaf tin with
clingfilm. Pour the mousse into the
prepared tin and chill for 2 hours until
set.
≈ Meanwhile, place the sauce
ingredients in a food processor and
liquidize until smooth. Press through a
sieve to discard the seeds. Unmould the
mousse on to a plate, remove the clingfilm, slice and serve with the sauce.

Vanilla Mousse ▶

BLUEBERRY CHEESECAKE

SERVES 6

A cheesecake with a delicious muesli and dried fig base, in place of the usual biscuits and butter, which gives a rich and crunchy base to the soft filling.

For the base

115 g (4 oz) muesli

150 g (5 oz) dried figs

For the filling

5 g (1 tsp) vegetarian gelatine

125 ml (4 fl oz) skimmed evaporated milk

1 egg

90 g (6 tbsp) caster sugar

450 g (1 lb) low-fat cottage cheese

50 g (2 oz) blueberries

For the topping

225 g (8 oz) blueberries

2 nectarines, pitted and sliced

30 ml (2 tbsp) honey

≈ Place the muesli and dried figs in a food processor and liquidize for 30 seconds. Press into the base of a base lined 20 cm (8 in) springform tin and chill while preparing the filling.

≈ Sprinkle the gelatine on to 60 ml (4 tablespoons) of cold water. Stir until dissolved and heat to boiling point. Boil for 2 minutes. Cool. Place the milk, egg, sugar and cheese in a food processor and liquidize until smooth. Stir in the blueberries. Place in a mixing bowl and gradually stir in the dissolved gelatine. Pour the mixture on to the base and chill for 2 hours until set.

≈ Remove the cheesecake from the pan and arrange the fruit for the topping in alternate rings on top. Drizzle the honey over the fruit and serve.

NUTRITION FACTS	
Serving Size 1 (238g)	
Calories 215	Calories from Fat 18
	% Daily Value
Total Fat 2g	3%
Saturated Fat 1g	4%
Monounsaturated Fat 0.6g	0%
Polyunsaturated Fat 0.2g	0%
Cholesterol 39mg	13%
Sodium 333mg	14%
Total Carbohydrate 40g	13%
Dietary Fibre 3g	13%
Sugars 44g	0%
Protein 13g	0%

Per cent daily values are based on a 2000 calorie diet

CRÈME CARAMEL

MAKES 4

Although low in fat, this recipe uses two whole eggs and should therefore follow a main course which does not use eggs to balance the fat content of the meal.

5 g (2 tsp) caster sugar

2 eggs, beaten

300 ml (½ pint) skimmed milk

2.5 ml (½ tsp) vanilla extract

dash of ground cinnamon

≈ Dissolve the 115 g (4 oz) sugar in a pan with 150 ml (¼ pint) cold water. Bring to the boil and boil rapidly until the mixture begins to turn golden brown. Pour into the base of 4 × 150 ml (¼ pint) ramekin dishes.

≈ Whisk the remaining sugar with the eggs in a bowl. Heat the milk with the vanilla and cinnamon until just boiling and gradually whisk into the egg mixture.

≈ Pour into the ramekins and place in a shallow roasting tin with enough hot water to reach halfway up the sides. Cover and cook in the oven at 180°C (350°F, Gas 4) for 50 minutes until set. Remove from the pan, slightly cool and chill in the refrigerator for 1 hour. Unmould on to individual plates and serve immediately.

Blueberry Cheesecake ▶

NUTRITION FACTS	
Serving Size 1 (130g)	
Calories 171	Calories from Fat 18
	% Daily Value
Total Fat 2g	4%
Saturated Fat 1g	4%
Monounsaturated Fat 1.0g	0%
Polyunsaturated Fat 0.3g	0%
Cholesterol 106mg	35%
Sodium 71mg	3%
Total Carbohydrate 32g	10%
Dietary Fibre 0g	0%
Sugars 30g	0%
Protein 6g	0%

Per cent daily values are based on a 2000 calorie diet

PLUM AND GINGER BRÛLÉE

SERVES 4

Plums and ginger are a great combination in this easy brûlée recipe, the ginger adding just enough spice to complement the plums.

≈ Spoon the plums into the base of 4 × 150 ml (¼ pint) ramekin dishes. Lightly whip the cream substitute and fold in the yogurt and ground ginger. Spoon on to the fruit and chill for 2 hours.

≈ Sprinkle the brown sugar on top of the yogurt mixture and grill for 5 minutes or until the sugar has dissolved. Chill for 20 minutes before serving.

---

4 plums, stoned and chopped

250 ml (8 fl oz) half-fat cream substitute

250 ml (8 fl oz) low-fat natural yogurt

2.5 g (½ tsp) ground ginger

60 g (4 tbsp) soft brown sugar

NUTRITION FACTS

Serving Size 1 (479g)

Calories 344	Calories from Fat 27
	% Daily Value
Total Fat 3g	4%
Saturated Fat 1g	4%
Monounsaturated Fat 1.4g	0%
Polyunsaturated Fat 0.4g	0%
Cholesterol 4mg	1%
Sodium 86mg	4%
Total Carbohydrate 74g	25%
Dietary Fibre 4g	14%
Sugars 46g	0%
Protein 8g	0%

Per cent daily values are based on a 2000 calorie diet

CAPPUCCINO SPONGES

SERVES 4

These individual sponge puddings are delicious served with the low-fat coffee sauce. Ideal for dinner parties, they look more delicate and attractive than one large pudding.

≈ Use non-stick spray to lightly grease 4 × 150 ml (¼ pint) individual pudding moulds. Cream the margarine and the sugar together in a bowl and add the egg whites. Sieve the flour and baking powder together and fold into the creamed mixture with a metal spoon. Gradually stir in the milk, coffee extract and cocoa.

≈ Spoon equal amounts of the mixture into the moulds. Cover with pleated greaseproof paper, then foil, and tie securely with string. Place in a steamer or pan with sufficient boiling water to reach halfway up the sides of the moulds. Cover and cook for 30 minutes or until cooked through.

≈ Meanwhile, place the milk, sugar, coffee extract and coffee liqueur in a pan to make the sauce. Blend the cornflour with 60 ml (4 tablespoons) of cold water and stir into the pan. Bring to the boil, stirring until thickened. Reduce the heat and cook for a further 2–3 minutes.

≈ Carefully remove the cooked puddings from the steamer. Remove the paper and foil and unmould on to individual plates. Spoon the sauce around and serve.

---

30 g (2 tbsp) polyunsaturated margarine

30 g (2 tbsp) soft brown sugar

2 egg whites

50 g (2 oz) plain flour

4 g (¾ tsp) baking powder

90 ml (6 tbsp) skimmed milk

5 ml (1 tsp) coffee extract

2.5 g (½ tsp) unsweetened cocoa powder

For the coffee sauce

300 ml (½ pint) skimmed milk

15 g (1 tbsp) soft brown sugar

5 ml (1 tsp) coffee extract

5 ml (1 tsp) coffee liqueur (optional)

30 g (2 tbsp) cornflour

NUTRITION FACTS

Serving Size 1 (154g)

Calories 199	Calories from Fat 54
	% Daily Value
Total Fat 6g	9%
Saturated Fat 1g	6%
Monounsaturated Fat 2.6g	0%
Polyunsaturated Fat 1.9g	0%
Cholesterol 2mg	1%
Sodium 241mg	10%
Total Carbohydrate 29g	10%
Dietary Fibre 1g	2%
Sugars 12g	0%
Protein 7g	0%

Per cent daily values are based on a 2000 calorie diet

Plum and Ginger Brûlée ▶

NUT, HONEY AND CINNAMON BAKLAVA PASTRIES

MAKES ABOUT 24

A mixture of walnuts and almonds is used in this version of the classic Greek pastry but if you prefer you can stick to one or the other – or indeed, try using pistachios instedd.

100 g/4 oz polyunsaturated
  margarine
450 g/1 lb filo pastry, thawed if
  frozen

Filling

4 tbsp clear honey
2 tbsp freshly squeezed lemon juice
50 g/2 oz caster sugar
2 tsp ground cinnamon
1 tsp finely grated lemon zest
100 g/4 oz blanched almonds,
  roughly chopped
100 g/4 oz shelled walnuts, roughly
  chopped

Syrup

400 g/14 oz caster sugar
5 tbsp clear honey
600 ml/1 pt water
1 cinnamon stick
strip of lemon peel

≈ Preheat the oven to 170°C/325°F/ Gas Mark 3. Grease a roasting pan. Trim the sheet of filo pastry dough to fit inside the pan and discard the trimmings.

≈ Place the first sheet of filo dough in the base of the prepared pan and brush evenly with melted margarine. Lay another sheet of filo on top and brush again with the melted margarine. Repeat this process until you have 12 sheets of filo pastry dough layered on the bottom of the pan. Cover the remaining filo pastry dough with a slightly damp cloth to prevent it from drying out while you work.

≈ To make the filling, place the honey in a medium-sized bowl. Add the lemon juice and stir until combined. Stir in the sugar, ground cinnamon, lemon zest and nuts. Spread half of the filling mixture over the filo in the base of the pan.

≈ Layer another three sheets of filo pastry dough on top of the filling, brushing each sheet with melted margarine. Spread the remaining filling mixture over the filo and cover with the remaining sheets of filo, brushing each sheet with melted margarine. Brush the top with any remaining margarine and score into 5 cm/2-inch diamond shapes. Bake for about 1 hour, or until crisp and golden. Remove from the oven and stand on a wire rack.

≈ To make the syrup, place all the ingredients together in a medium-sized saucepan and heat gently until the sugar has dissolved completely. Increase the heat and boil rapidly for about 10 minutes, without stirring. Set aside to cool. Discard the cinnamon stick and lemon peel and pour the syrup evenly over the pastry.

NUTRITION FACTS	
Amount per Serving (each)	
Calories 185	Calories from Fat 100
	% Daily Value
Total Fat 11g	17%
Saturated Fat 1.5g	7.5%
Polyunsaturated Fat 5g	0%
Monounsaturated Fat 4g	0%
Cholesterol 0mg	0%
Sodium 40mg	2%
Total Carbohydrate 20g	7%
Dietary Fibre 1g	4%
Sugars 8g	0%
Protein 4g	0%

Percent daily values are based on a 2000 calorie diet

450 g/1 lb kumquats, washed and
cut into thin slices

225 g/8 oz sugar

150 ml/5 fl oz cold water

150 ml/5 fl oz warm water

25 g/1 oz seedless raisins

Decoration

bay leaf

NUTRITION FACTS	
Amount per Serving	
Calories 284	Calories from Fat 0
	% Daily Value
Total Fat 0g	0%
Saturated Fat 0g	0%
Polyunsaturated Fat 0g	0%
Monounsaturated Fat 0g	0%
Cholesterol 0mg	0%
Sodium 14mg	0.5%
Total Carbohydrate 64g	21%
Dietary Fibre 6g	24%
Sugars 64g	0%
Protein 1g	0%

Percent daily values are based on a 2000 calorie diet

KUMQUATS IN CARAMEL

SERVES 4

Smallest of all the citrus fruits, kumquats are a good source of vitamins A and C, potassium, magnesium and calcium. Sliced and arranged in rings they make an unusual garnish. Their characteristic tartness is offset in this recipe by a delicious golden caramel sauce.

≈ Put the sugar and cold water into a medium-sized, heavy-based pan. Dissolve the sugar slowly over low heat, stirring occasionally. Bring to the boil and boil steadily until caramel coloured (about 5 minutes).

≈ Remove the pan from the heat and leave it to cool a little. Gradually pour on the warm water, taking great care that the sugar mixture does not splash.

≈ Return the pan to low heat to dissolve the caramel, then remove it from the heat and allow to cool.

≈ Arrange the sliced kumquats in a serving dish, and scatter the raisins over them. Pour the caramel over the fruit. Decorate with the bay leaf and serve chilled.

2 tbsp clear honey

1 tbsp lemon juice

4 tbsp orange juice

4 ripe figs, sliced into rings

2 oranges, peeled and segmented

4 sprigs of mint

NUTRITION FACTS	
Amount per Serving	
Calories 80	Calories from Fat 0
	% Daily Value
Total Fat 0g	0%
Saturated Fat 0g	0%
Polyunsaturated Fat 0g	0%
Monounsaturated Fat 0g	0%
Cholesterol 0mg	0%
Sodium 7mg	0.3%
Total Carbohydrate 19g	6%
Dietary Fibre 3g	12%
Sugars 19g	0%
Protein 2g	0%

Percent daily values are based on a 2000 calorie diet

HONEY AND ORANGE FIGS

SERVES 4

This recipe offers a refreshing way to serve fresh figs.

≈ Stir the honey into the fruit juices until it has dissolved. Put the fruit into a dish, pour the honey mixture over the fruit and stir lightly. Cover and chill for at least 1 hour.

≈ Stir gently before dividing among 4 chilled dishes. Decorate each serving with a sprig of mint.

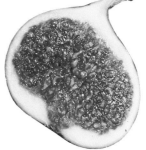

WATERMELON GRANITÉ

SERVES 8

1 medium-sized watermelon

50 g/2 oz icing sugar

150 ml/5 fl oz ginger ale

1 tbsp lemon or lime juice

NUTRITION FACTS	
Amount per Serving	
Calories 66	Calories from Fat 0
	% Daily Value
Total Fat 0g	0%
Saturated Fat 0g	0%
Polyunsaturated Fat 0g	0%
Monounsaturated Fat 0g	0%
Cholesterol 0mg	0%
Sodium 3mg	0.1%
Total Carbohydrate 17g	6%
Dietary Fibre 1g	4%
Sugars 17g	0%
Protein 0.3g	0%

Percent daily values are based on a 2000 calorie diet

≈ Cut into the top of the watermelon in a zig-zag pattern, then lift the top off carefully.

≈ Using a spoon, scoop out the flesh and remove all the seeds. Freeze the shell. Place the flesh in a blender in batches and blend until smooth. Pour into a bowl.

≈ Dissolve the icing sugar in the ginger ale, stir in the lemon or lime juice and add to the melon. Pour into a suitable container. Freeze until ice crystals form around the edges, then draw these into the mixture. Freeze until the whole is a mass of small crystals. Scrape into the reserved shell and serve.

TANGERINE AND GINGER SORBET

SERVES 8

8 large tangerines

1 cm/½ in piece fresh ginger, peeled
and grated

175 g/6 oz caster sugar

finely grated peel and juice of
1 lemon

finely grated peel and juice of
1 small orange

finely grated peel and juice of
½ grapefruit

1 egg white

≈ Cut the tops off the tangerines and reserve. Using a grapefruit knife, cut out the fruit. Place the empty shells in tartlet pans. Remove the seeds from the fruit and blend the pulp with the ginger. Strain into a saucepan, add the sugar and heat until dissolved. Add the grated peel and juice of the lemon, orange and grapefruit. Put into a container suitable for the freezer and freeze until just firm. Remove from the freezer and beat.

≈ Whisk the egg white until stiff and fold into the frozen mixture. Spoon into the empty shells, top each with the reserved lids, return these to the tartlet pans and freeze until firm.

NUTRITION FACTS	
Amount per Serving	
Calories 99	Calories from Fat 0
	% Daily Value
Total Fat 0g	0%
Saturated Fat 0g	0%
Polyunsaturated Fat 0g	0%
Monounsaturated Fat 0g	0%
Cholesterol 0mg	0%
Sodium 12mg	0.5%
Total Carbohydrate 25g	8%
Dietary Fibre 1g	4%
Sugars 25g	0%
Protein 1g	0%

Percent daily values are based on a 2000 calorie diet

FRESH FRUIT DESSERT CAKE

SERVES 8

2 eggs

50 ml/2 fl oz milk

2 tbsp honey

2 tbsp treacle

175 g/6 oz wholemeal flour

1 tsp baking powder

1 tsp bicarbonate of soda

1 tsp cinnamon

pinch of salt

450 g/1 lb peaches

225 g/½ lb plums

225 g/½ lb cherries

100 g/4 oz walnuts, chopped

a little margarine

fresh fruit to decorate

To serve

whipped cream*

≈ Preheat the oven to 200°C/400°F/ Gas Mark 6.

≈ Beat the eggs with the milk. Stir in the honey and treacle. Stir in the rest of the dry ingredients and mix well.

≈ Remove the stones and chop the fruit. Mix it into the batter with the nuts. Pour into a greased and floured 20 cm/ 8 inch cake pan with a removable bottom (spring form cake pan) and bake for 50–60 minutes until set in the middle. Dot with margarine towards the end of the cooking time to prevent the top drying out.

≈ Allow to cool in the pan. Chill and decorate with fresh fruit.

NUTRITION FACTS

Amount per Serving

Calories 240	Calories from Fat 100

	% Daily Value
Total Fat 11g	17%
Saturated Fat 1g	5%
Polyunsaturated Fat 6g	0%
Monounsaturated Fat 2g	0%
Cholesterol 60mg	20%
Sodium 31mg	1%
Total Carbohydrate 30g	10%
Dietary Fibre 5.5g	22%
Sugars 16g	0%
Protein 8g	0%

Percent daily values are based on a 2000 calorie diet

GRAPE CUSTARDS

SERVES 4

225 g/½ lb seedless red grapes

4 egg yolks

3 tbsp caster sugar

4 tbsp marsala, madeira, or sweet
   sherry

NUTRITION FACTS	
Amount per Serving	
Calories 174	Calories from Fat 54
	% Daily Value
Total Fat 6g	9%
Saturated Fat 2g	10%
Polyunsaturated Fat 1g	0%
Monounsaturated Fat 2g	0%
Cholesterol 202mg	67%
Sodium 13mg	0.5%
Total Carbohydrate 25g	8%
Dietary Fibre 0.5g	2%
Sugars 25g	0%
Protein 3g	0%

Percent daily values are based on a 2000 calorie diet

≈ Wash the grapes and divide among 4 individual glasses.

≈ Place the egg yolks in a bowl. Beat lightly, add the sugar and wine and mix together. Place the bowl over a pan of hot water and whisk, for about 10 minutes, until the mixture is thick and creamy.

≈ Divide the mixture among the glasses and serve at once while still warm with sponge fingers.

LYCHEE AND LIME SORBET

SERVES 4

450 g/1 lb fresh lychees

juice of 1 lime

25 g/1 oz icing sugar, sifted

1 egg white

≈ Peel the lychees and remove the stones. Place the flesh in a blender with the lime juice and icing sugar. Process until smooth.

≈ Pour into a container suitable for the freezer, freeze until slushy, then beat well. Repeat this twice.

≈ Whisk the egg white until firm and fold into the sorbet. Freeze for several hours until solid.

≈ Serve in small scoops with slices of fresh mango or other suitable fruit, or with another fruit sorbet such as mango or kiwi.

NUTRITION FACTS	
Amount per Serving	
Calories 201	Calories from Fat 0
	% Daily Value
Total Fat 0g	0%
Saturated Fat 0g	0%
Polyunsaturated Fat 0g	0%
Monounsaturated Fat 0g	0%
Cholesterol 0mg	0%
Sodium 18mg	0.75%
Total Carbohydrate 52g	17%
Dietary Fibre 1g	4%
Sugars 52g	0%
Protein 2g	0%

Percent daily values are based on a 2000 calorie diet

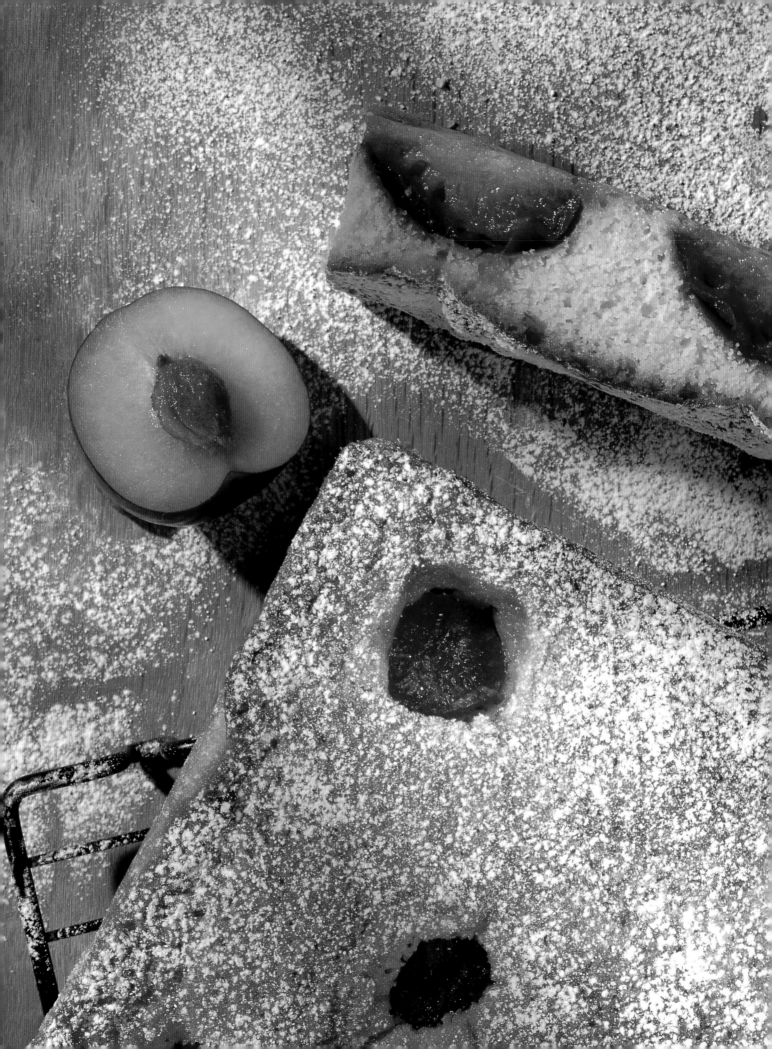

BAKED GOODS

SWEET SPICED FIG BREAD

MAKES ONE 1 LB (450 G) LOAF

Not so much a bread as a spiced tea bread which is especially good with cottage cheese and orange segments.

5 oz (140 g) wholemeal flour

2 tsp baking powder

1 tsp ground cinnamon

large pinch grated nutmeg

6 oz (180 g) rolled oats

3 oz (85 g) light Muscovado or
    brown sugar

3 tbsp clear honey

10 fl oz (300 ml) skimmed milk

4 oz (115 g) dried figs, chopped

NUTRITION FACTS	
Amount per Serving (per loaf)	
Calories 1510	Calories from Fat 135
	% Daily Value
Total Fat 15g	20%
Saturated Fat 2.5g	12.5%
Polyunsaturated Fat 5g	0%
Monounsaturated Fat 4g	0%
Cholesterol 6mg	2%
Sodium 273mg	10%
Total Carbohydrate 330g	1%
Dietary Fibre 33.5g	132%
Sugars 196g	0%
Protein 39g	0%

Percent daily values are based on a 2000 calorie diet

≈ Preheat the oven to 180°C/350°F/ Gas 4. Sift the flour, baking powder and spices into a bowl, and tip in any bran (husk) remaining in the sifter. Stir in the oats, sugar, and honey, then gradually pour on the milk, beating constantly. Stir in the chopped figs.

≈ Line a 1-lb (450-g) loaf tin with waxed paper, spoon in the mixture, and level the top. Bake in the oven for 50 minutes or until a skewer inserted into the loaf comes out clean.

≈ Leave the loaf to cool slightly in the pan, then turn it out onto a cake rack. When completely cool it can be wrapped in foil and stored in an airtight container.

DATE AND ORANGE BARS

MAKES 10 BARS

The zing of oranges and the sweetness of the dates make an irresistible combination.

8 oz (225 g) pitted dates, chopped

grated rind of 2 oranges

1 orange, peeled, sectioned, and
  chopped

2 oz (60 g) polyunsaturated
  margarine

6 oz (180 g) rolled oats

4 oz (115 g) wholemeal flour

3 tbsp clear honey

2 oz (60 g) pecan nuts, chopped

1 tbsp sesame seeds

oil, for brushing

≈ Preheat the oven to 180°C/375°F/ Gas 5. Mix together the dates, orange rind and chopped orange, and set aside.

≈ Melt the margarine in a small pan and stir in the oats, flour, honey, nuts and seeds. Lightly oil a 7-inch square cake tin.

≈ Press half the oat mixture into the tin to cover the base. Level the surface and cover it with the date mixture. Spread the remaining oat mixture on top, and press it down evenly.

≈ Bake in the oven for 25–30 minutes, until the top is golden brown. Cool slightly, then cut into ten bars. To do this, cut the cake in half, and then cut each half into five bars.

NUTRITION FACTS	
Amount per Serving (per bar)	
Calories 196	Calories from Fat 80
	% Daily Value
Total Fat 9g	0.1%
Saturated Fat 1.5g	7.5%
Polyunsaturated Fat 3.5g	0%
Monounsaturated Fat 3g	0%
Cholesterol 0mg	0%
Sodium 43mg	2%
Total Carbohydrate 28g	9%
Dietary Fibre 3g	12%
Sugars 17g	0%
Protein 3g	0%

Percent daily values are based on a 2000 calorie diet

LOW-FAT SPONGECAKE

MAKES 6 SLICES

For this classic sponge cake, no butter, margarine or oil is used in the mixture. It must be noted, however, that the use of three egg yolks contributes a significant cholesterol content. An electric beater is a great advantage.

oil, for brushing

3 large eggs

3 oz (85 g) caster sugar

few drops vanilla essence

4 oz (115 g) plain flour, plus extra for dusting

Filling

4 oz (115 g) strawberry jam

4 oz (115 g) low-fat yogurt

Topping

3 tbsp icing sugar

≈ Preheat the oven to 180°C/350°F/ Gas 4. First prepare the tins. Lightly brush the bases of two 7-in (18-cm) diameter cake tins with oil. Line the base of each pan with a circle of waxed paper, and brush that with oil. Dust the base and sides of each tin with flour. Shake off excess flour.

≈ Pour boiling water into a saucepan to a depth of 2 in (5 cm), and fit a large ovenproof bowl over it. Put the pan on low heat to keep the water simmering.

≈ Put the eggs, sugar and vanilla essence into the bowl and whisk until the mixture is very thick and warm. A hand-held electric beater will take about 10 minutes.

≈ Remove the bowl from the heat and beat until the beaters leave a trail in the mixture and it has cooled.

≈ Gradually sift the flour, a little at a time, into the egg mixture, folding it in with a metal spoon. Divide the mixture between the two pans, and level the tops.

≈ Bake in the oven for 20–25 minutes, until the cakes have shrunk away from the sides of the tins.

≈ Leave the cakes in the tins for about 5 minutes, then turn them out onto cake racks. Peel off the paper and leave them to cool. When the cakes are cool, sandwich them together with the jam and yogurt.

JELLY ROLL

≈ You can use this mixture to make a jelly roll. Brush the tin with oil, line it with waxed paper, and brush that with oil.

≈ When the cake is cooled, turn it out onto a sheet of waxed paper sprinkled with fine granulated sugar. Place another sheet of paper on top and roll up the cake with the paper inside.

≈ Unroll the cake when it is cool, remove the paper, and spread the cake with jam or jelly. Roll it up again and sprinkle with icing sugar.

NUTRITION FACTS	
Amount per Serving (per slice)	
Calories 237	Calories from Fat 36
	% Daily Value
Total Fat 4g	6%
Saturated Fat 1g	5%
Polyunsaturated Fat 1g	0%
Monounsaturated Fat 2g	0%
Cholesterol 120mg	40%
Sodium 73mg	3%
Total Carbohydrate 47g	16%
Dietary Fibre 0.5g	2%
Sugars 39g	0%
Protein 6g	0%

Percent daily values are based on a 2000 calorie diet

HERBED SCONES

MAKES ABOUT 10 SCONES

These savoury scones, eaten warm, make a good snack to enjoy with low-fat cheese or grapes and celery. They also make a good accompaniment to a bowl of steaming hot soup.

7½ oz (210 g) wholemeal flour, plus
    extra for dusting

½ tsp salt

¼ tsp bicarbonate of soda

2 oz (60 g) polyunsaturated
    margarine

1 tsp mixed dry herbs

1 tsp paprika

6 oz (180 g) plain low-fat yogurt or
    buttermilk

milk, to glaze

≈ Preheat the oven to 205°C/400°F/ Gas 6. Sift the flour, salt and soda into a bowl. Rub in the margarine until the mixture resembles fine bread crumbs. Stir in the herbs and paprika, and make a well in the centre of the dry ingredients. Mix in the yogurt or buttermilk to make a firm dough.
≈ Turn out the dough on to a lightly-floured board, and knead it lightly to remove any cracks. Roll it out to a thickness of about ¾ in (2 cm), then, using a fluted cutter, cut it into 2 in (5 cm) circles. Re-roll the trimmings and cut into more circles. Brush the tops with milk to glaze.
≈ Place the scones on a non-stick baking tray, and bake in the oven for 20 minutes, until they are well risen and golden brown. Transfer the scones to a cake rack to cool slightly. Serve warm.

NUTRITION FACTS

Amount per Serving (per biscuit)

Calories 104	Calories from Fat 45
	% Daily Value
Total Fat 5g	8%
Saturated Fat 1g	5%
Polyunsaturated Fat 2g	0%
Monounsaturated Fat 1.5g	0%
Cholesterol 1mg	0.3%
Sodium 51mg	2%
Total Carbohydrate 12g	4%
Dietary Fibre 2g	8%
Sugars 1.5g	0%
Protein 3g	0%

Percent daily values are based on a 2000 calorie diet

COCONUT MACAROONS

MAKES ABOUT 30

Macaroons taste delicious and are a good way to use extra egg whites.

4 egg whites

¼ tsp cream of tartar

5 oz (140 g) sugar

1 tsp lemon juice or distilled white
    vinegar

1 tsp vanilla essence

10 oz (285 g) moist, unsweetened
    shredded coconut

≈ In a large bowl, with electric mixer at medium speed, beat whites until frothy. Add cream of tartar and beat on high speed until firm peaks form. Gradually sprinkle in sugar, 2 tablespoons at a time, beating well after each addition until whites form stiff peaks.

≈ Sprinkle lemon juice or vinegar, vanilla and coconut over whites. Gently fold in until just blended.

≈ Preheat oven to 150°C/300°F/Gas 2. Line 2 large baking trays with nonstick parchment paper or foil. Drop mixture by heaping teaspoonfuls, keeping a cone shape, about 1 inch apart.

≈ Bake 40–45 minutes until lightly browned; macaroons should be *very* slightly soft in centre. Carefully peel off paper and cool completely. Store in an airtight container.

NUTRITION FACTS	
Amount per Serving (each)	
Calories 47	Calories from Fat 18
	% Daily Value
Total Fat 2g	3%
Saturated Fat 2g	10%
Polyunsaturated Fat 0.05g	0%
Monounsaturated Fat 0.1g	0%
Cholesterol 0mg	0%
Sodium 9mg	0.4%
Total Carbohydrate 7g	2%
Dietary Fibre 0.5g	2%
Sugars 7g	0%
Protein 0.5g	0%

Percent daily values are based on a 2000 calorie diet

8 oz (225 g) finely ground blanched
    almonds or walnuts

7 oz (200 g) sugar

1 tbsp ground cinnamon

2 egg whites

⅛ tsp cream of tartar

icing sugar and cinnamon for rolling

NUTRITION FACTS	
Amount per Serving (each)	
Calories 97	Calories from Fat 54
	% Daily Value
Total Fat 6g	9%
Saturated Fat 0.5g	2.5%
Polyunsaturated Fat 1g	0%
Monounsaturated Fat 3g	0%
Cholesterol 0mg	0%
Sodium 8mg	0.3%
Total Carbohydrate 10g	3%
Dietary Fibre 1g	4%
Sugars 10g	0%
Protein 2g	0%

Percent daily values are based on a 2000 calorie diet

EASY CINNAMON BALLS

MAKES ABOUT 20

These biscuits are so easy children can make them. Children should not go close to the oven and may not produce uniform results, but they will have a good time. If mixture is too soft to roll, add a little more ground almond to stiffen it.

≈ Preheat oven to 165°C/325°F/Gas 3. Lightly grease a large baking tray. In a medium bowl, combine ground almonds or walnuts, half the sugar and cinnamon. Set aside.

≈ In another medium bowl, with electric mixer, beat whites until frothy. Add cream of tartar and continue beating until soft peaks form. Gradually add remaining sugar, 1 tablespoonful at a time, beating well after each addition, until whites are stiff and glossy. Gently fold in nut mixture.

≈ With wet hands, shape mixture into walnut-size balls. Place on baking sheet about 1-in (2.5-cm) apart. Bake until golden brown and set, 25–30 minutes. Remove baking sheet to wire rack to cool slightly.

≈ In a small bowl, combine icing sugar and ¼ teaspoon cinnamon until well blended. Roll each warm ball in mixture to coat, then set on wire rack to cool completely. Add more icing sugar and cinnamon if necessary. When cold, roll each ball again in sugar mixture.

8 oz (225 g) raisins

6 oz (180 g) dried apricots, chopped

1 egg, beaten

2 tbsp polyunsaturated margarine,
    melted with 2 tbsp hot water

8 oz (225 g) muesli

1 heaped tbsp chopped nuts

NUTRITION FACTS	
Amount per Serving (per cookie)	
Calories 169	Calories from Fat 54
	% Daily Value
Total Fat 6g	9%
Saturated Fat 2g	10%
Polyunsaturated Fat 1g	0%
Monounsaturated Fat 02	0%
Cholesterol 30mg	10%
Sodium 192mg	8%
Total Carbohydrate 26g	9%
Dietary Fibre 3g	12%
Sugars 12g	0%
Protein 5g	0%

Percent daily values are based on a 2000 calorie diet

MUESLI COOKIES

MAKES 10

≈ Preheat the oven to 180°C/350°F/Gas 4.

≈ Pick over dried fruit and wash in boiling water. Drain. Put fruit in a bowl and beat well with egg and butter. Stir in muesli and nuts.

≈ Line a baking tray with greased waxed paper and spread the mixture thinly over it. Mark into bars and bake for 45 minutes.

≈ Cut bars through and allow to cool for 10 minutes before removing from the tray. Finish cooling on a wire rack.

PUMPKIN, SUNFLOWER SEED AND RAISIN CAKE

MAKES 10–12 SLICES

1 lb (450 g) pumpkin

12 oz (340 g) wholemeal flour

pinch of salt

2 tsp baking powder

1 tsp bicarbonate of soda

2 oz (60 g) sunflower seeds, chopped

2 oz (60 g) raisins

2 eggs

2 tbsp honey

2 tbsp treacle

1 tbsp warm water

NUTRITION FACTS	
Amount per Serving (per slice)	
Calories 126	Calories from Fat 36
	% Daily Value
Total Fat 4g	6%
Saturated Fat 0.5g	2.5%
Polyunsaturated Fat 2g	0%
Monounsaturated Fat 1g	0%
Cholesterol 40mg	13%
Sodium 18mg	0.75%
Total Carbohydrate 20g	7%
Dietary Fibre 3g	12%
Sugars 6g	0%
Protein 5g	0%

Percent daily values are based on a 2000 calorie diet

≈ Preheat the oven to 190°C/375°F/ Gas 5. Peel the pumpkin, cut into smallish pieces and boil until tender. Drain and cut up finely.

≈ Combine flour, salt, baking powder, sunflower seeds and raisins and mix well.

≈ In another bowl, beat the eggs and stir in the honey and treacle. Add 1 tablespoon of warm water with the pumpkin and beat well.

≈ Mix all the ingredients together thoroughly and pour into a greased and floured pan. Bake for 50–60 minutes until done. Allow to stand for 10 minutes in the pan, then cool on a wire rack.

BANANA, NECTARINE AND ALMOND LOAF

MAKES 10–12 SLICES

10 oz (280 g) wholemeal flour

3 oz (85 g) wheatgerm

2 oz (60 g) dried nectarines, chopped

2 oz (60 g) almonds, chopped

2 tsp baking powder

1 tsp bicarbonate of soda

pinch of salt

2 tbsp honey

2 tbsp treacle

½ tsp vanilla

3 bananas, mashed

1 egg, beaten

≈ Preheat the oven to 180°C/350°F/Gas 4.

≈ Mix the dry ingredients together in a large bowl. Mix the remaining ingredients together thoroughly in another bowl, then combine the two and stir well.

· ≈ Tip into a greased and floured loaf pan 4 × 9 in (10 × 23 cm), and bake for about 50 minutes, or until a toothpick inserted in the middle of the loaf comes out cleanly. Allow to cool for 15 minutes, then tip out of the pan and cool completely on a wire rack before cutting. Eat it on its own or spread it with low-fat spread or cream cheese.

NUTRITION FACTS	
Amount per Serving (per slice)	
Calories 134	Calories from Fat 27
	% Daily Value
Total Fat 3g	5%
Saturated Fat 0.5g	2.5%
Polyunsaturated Fat 1g	0%
Monounsaturated Fat 1.5g	0%
Cholesterol 20mg	7%
Sodium 10mg	0.4%
Total Carbohydrate 23g	8%
Dietary Fibre 4g	16%
Sugars 10g	0%
Protein 5g	0%

Percent daily values are based on a 2000 calorie diet

ANGEL CAKE

SERVES 12

Although it sounds complicated, this recipe is very easy to make. Be sure to treat the mixture gently so as not to beat out all of the air.

3 eggs

90 g (6 tbsp) caster sugar

25 g (1 oz) self raising flour

few drops of pink food colouring

few drops of yellow food colouring

For the filling

225 g (8 oz) low-fat soft cheese,
     such as curd or cream cheese

30 g (2 tbsp) icing sugar

NUTRITION FACTS	
Serving Size 1 (28g)	
Calories 74	Calories from Fat 9
	% Daily Value
Total Fat 1g	2%
Saturated Fat 0g	2%
Monounsaturated Fat 0.5g	0%
Polyunsaturated Fat 0.2g	0%
Cholesterol 53mg	18%
Sodium 115mg	5%
Total Carbohydrate 13g	4%
Dietary Fibre 0g	1%
Sugars 7g	0%
Protein 2g	0%

Per cent daily values are based on a 2000 calorie diet

≈ Line 3 × 900 g (2 lb) loaf tins with non-stick baking paper. Whisk the eggs and sugar in a large bowl until thick and pale and the whisk leaves a trail in the mixture when lifted. Sieve the flour into the mixture and fold in gently.

≈ Divide the mixture into three equal quantities and place in separate bowls. Add a few drops of pink colouring to one bowl and stir in gently. Add a few drops of yellow food colouring to another bowl and stir in gently.

≈ Spoon the pink mixture into one prepared tin, the yellow into another and the plain mixture into the third. Bake in the oven at 200°C (400°F, Gas 6) for 10 minutes until the mixture springs back when gently pressed. Turn out and cool completely on a wire rack.

≈ Trim the sides from each cake. Mix together the filling ingredients. Place the yellow cake on a chopping board and spread half of the filling on top. Place the pink cake on top and spread with the remaining filling. Top with the white cake. Dust with icing sugar and slice to serve.

GINGERBREAD

SERVES 16

Skimmed milk, prunes and egg white are used in this classic cake to reduce the fat content. For an extra spicy flavour, add 15 g (1 teaspoon) of ground allspice to the mixture as well as the ginger.

450 g (1 lb) plain flour

dash of salt

15 g (1 tbsp) ground ginger

15 g (1 tbsp) baking powder

5 ml (1 tsp) bicarbonate of soda

175 g (6 oz) soft brown sugar

185 g (6½ oz) molasses

150 ml (5 fl oz) golden syrup

115 g (4 oz) dried stoned prunes

300 ml (½ pint) skimmed milk

1 egg white

icing sugar for dusting

2 pieces stem ginger, chopped

NUTRITION FACTS	
Serving Size 1 (107g)	
Calories 267	Calories from Fat 0
	% Daily Value
Total Fat 0g	1%
Saturated Fat 0g	0%
Monounsaturated Fat 0.0g	0%
Polyunsaturated Fat 0.1g	0%
Cholesterol 0mg	0%
Sodium 231mg	10%
Total Carbohydrate 62g	21%
Dietary Fibre 2g	6%
Sugars 23g	0%
Protein 4g	0%

Per cent daily values are based on a 2000 calorie diet

≈ Grease and line a 23 cm (9 in) square tin. Sift the flour, salt, ground ginger, baking powder and soda into a large bowl.

≈ Place the sugar, molasses and syrup in a pan and heat gently to dissolve. Place the prunes in a food processor with 45 ml (3 tablespoons) of water and liquidize for 30 seconds until puréed. Add the milk to the sugar mixture and stir into the dry ingredients with the prunes. Whisk the egg white until peaking, fold into the mixture and spoon into the prepared tin.

≈ Bake in the oven at 160°C (325°F, Gas 3) for 55 minutes–1 hour or until firm. Cool in the pan for 10 minutes. Turn the cake out on to a wire rack and cool completely. Cut into 16 pieces. Dust with icing sugar and top with chopped ginger.

Gingerbread ▶

CHOCOLATE BROWNIES

MAKES 16

Chocolate brownies in a low-fat book? They taste just as good as the real thing but have a slightly different texture. Keep in an airtight container if you can resist them for long enough.

115 g (4 oz) stoned dried prunes

115 g (4 oz) soft brown sugar

45 g (3 tbsp) unsweetened cocoa powder, sieved

50 g (2 oz) plain flour

5 g (1 tsp) baking powder

3 egg whites

icing sugar for dusting

≈ Grease and line a shallow 18 cm (7 in) square cake tin.

≈ Place the prunes in a food processor with 45 ml (3 tablespoons) of water and liquidize to a purée. Transfer the purée to a mixing bowl and stir in the sugar, cocoa, flour and baking powder. Whisk the egg whites until peaking and fold into the mixture. Pour into the prepared tin and level the surface.

≈ Bake in the oven at 180°C (350°F, Gas 4) for 1 hour or until cooked through. Let the brownies cool in the tin for 10 minutes, then turn out on to a wire rack and cool completely. Cut into 16 squares, dust with icing sugar and serve.

NUTRITION FACTS

Serving Size 1 (36g)

Calories 90 — Calories from Fat 0

% Daily Value

Total Fat 0g	0%
Saturated Fat 0g	0%
Monounsaturated Fat 0.0g	0%
Polyunsaturated Fat 0.0g	0%
Cholesterol 0mg	0%
Sodium 45mg	2%
Total Carbohydrate 22g	7%
Dietary Fibre 1g	3%
Sugars 17g	0%
Protein 1g	0%

Per cent daily values are based on a 2000 calorie diet

SEED BREAD

SERVES 12

The seeds in this loaf add flavour and texture to the bread. Easy to eat, it is divided into six portions which are simply broken off for serving.

1 packet active dry yeast

450 g (1 lb) wholemeal flour

10 g (2 tsp) caster sugar

10 g (2 tsp) salt

30 g (2 tbsp) polyunsaturated margarine

10 g (2 tsp) caraway seeds

10 g (2 tsp) fennel seeds

10 g (2 tsp) sesame seeds

1 egg white

≈ Place the yeast, flour, sugar and salt in a large bowl. Rub in the margarine and add half of each of the seeds. Stir in 300 ml (½ pint) tepid water and mix well. Bring the mixture together to form a soft dough. Knead the dough for 5 minutes on a lightly floured surface and break into six equal pieces.

≈ Lightly grease a deep 15 cm (6 in) round cake tin. Shape each of the dough pieces into a round. Place five pieces around the edge of the tin and one in the centre. Cover and leave to prove in a warm place for 1 hour or until doubled in size.

≈ Whisk the egg white and brush over the top of the dough. Sprinkle the remaining seeds on to the top of the dough, alternating the different types on each section of the loaf.

≈ Bake in the oven at 200°C (400°F, Gas 6) for 30 minutes or until cooked through. The loaf should sound hollow when tapped on the base. Cool slightly and serve.

NUTRITION FACTS

Serving Size 1 (48g)

Calories 161 — Calories from Fat 27

% Daily Value

Total Fat 3g	5%
Saturated Fat 1g	3%
Monounsaturated Fat 1.0g	0%
Polyunsaturated Fat 0.9g	0%
Cholesterol 0mg	0%
Sodium 418mg	17%
Total Carbohydrate 30g	10%
Dietary Fibre 5g	21%
Sugars 1g	0%
Protein 6g	0%

Per cent daily values are based on a 2000 calorie diet

Seed Bread ▶

PEAR UPSIDE-DOWN CAKE

SERVES 8

In this recipe, sliced pears are set on a caramel base and topped with a spicy sponge mixture. Once cooked, turn out and serve immediately with natural yogurt.

30 ml (2 tbsp) honey

30 g (2 tbsp) soft brown sugar

2 large pears, peeled, cored and sliced

60 g (4 tbsp) polyunsaturated margarine

50 g (2 oz) caster sugar

3 egg whites

115 g (4 oz) self raising flour

10 g (2 tsp) ground allspice

≈ Heat the honey and sugar in a pan until melted. Pour into a base lined 20 cm (8 in) round cake tin. Arrange the pears around the base of the tin.

≈ Cream the margarine and sugar together until light and fluffy. Whisk the egg whites until peaking and fold into the mixture with the flour and allspice. Spoon on top of the pears.

≈ Bake in the oven at 180°C (350°F, Gas 4) for 50 minutes or until risen and golden. Stand for 5 minutes, then turn out on to a serving plate. Remove the lining paper and serve.

≈ Decorate with walnuts, but remember that nuts are high in fat and are best saved for special occasions.

NUTRITION FACTS

Serving Size 1 (92g)

Calories 190	Calories from Fat 54
	% Daily Value
Total Fat 6g	9%
Saturated Fat 1g	6%
Monounsaturated Fat 2.6g	0%
Polyunsaturated Fat 1.9g	0%
Cholesterol 0mg	0%
Sodium 287mg	12%
Total Carbohydrate 32g	11%
Dietary Fibre 2g	6%
Sugars 18g	0%
Protein 3g	0%

Per cent daily values are based on a 2000 calorie diet

ROCKY MOUNTAIN BUNS

MAKES 12

There is a hint of coffee in these fun-to-eat small buns. The marshmallows and sultanas give them a "rocky," uneven appearance.

275 g (10 oz) self raising flour

2.5 g (½ tsp) salt

50 g (2 oz) polyunsaturated margarine

30 g (2 tbsp) caster sugar

45 g (3 tbsp) sultanas

25 g (1 oz) mini marshmallows

150 ml (¼ pint) skimmed milk

15 ml (1 tbsp) coffee extract

icing sugar for dusting

≈ Sieve the flour and salt into a bowl. Rub in the margarine until the mixture resembles breadcrumbs. Stir in the sugar, sultanas and marshmallows.

≈ Mix together the milk and coffee extract and stir into the mixture to form a soft dough. Place 12 equal-sized spoonfuls of mixture on a non-stick baking sheet, spacing slightly apart.

≈ Bake in the oven at 220°C (425°F, Gas 7) for 20 minutes until risen and golden. Cool on a wire rack and serve.

NUTRITION FACTS

Serving Size 1 (58g)

Calories 172	Calories from Fat 36
	% Daily Value
Total Fat 4g	6%
Saturated Fat 1g	4%
Monounsaturated Fat 1.7g	0%
Polyunsaturated Fat 1.3g	0%
Cholesterol 0mg	0%
Sodium 481mg	20%
Total Carbohydrate 30g	10%
Dietary Fibre 1g	4%
Sugars 10g	0%
Protein 3g	0%

Per cent daily values are based on a 2000 calorie diet

Pear Upside-down Cake ▶

INDEX